FREE THINGS FOR HOMEOWNERS

BY YOLANDE FLESCH

CORNERSTONE LIBRARY
Published by Simon & Schuster
NEW YORK

Manufactured in the United States of America
10 9 8 7 6 5 4 3 2 1
Library of Congress Catalog Number: 80-70714
ISBN 0-346-12533-2

Table of Contents

Introduction
I. Buying, Building, and Renting
II. General Home Maintenance
III. Walls, Floors, and Ceilings
IV. Furniture, Appliances, and Accessories
V. Specific Rooms and Areas
VI. Exterior and Structural Maintenance
VII. Outdoor Places and Accessories
VIII. Tools, Paints, and Other Materials
IX. Energy Conservation
X. Heating and Insulation
XI. Health and Safety
XII. Finances and Family Records
XIII. Crafts and Hobbies

Special thanks for the editorial assistance of Mary Dennis and Houston Home/Garden Magazine.

INTRODUCTION

Y ou are about to discover over 225 free things and "almost free" things for homeowners: invaluable sources of projects, products, advice, tips, and suggestions for remodeling, repairing, or simply maintaining the present life of your home. This handbook of booklets and pamphlets available free (or for a nominal charge to cover postage and handling) will introduce you to imaginative yet practical ways to enhance your homelife, whether you are thinking about buying or building a new house, searching for an older one to renovate yourself, or whether you merely want to fix up the attic of your present home for a teenager's bedroom or add a cedar closet or a weather vane. Also included are sections on energy conservation, keeping valuable family records, home safety, and the hobbies and crafts that enrich a family's many hours together.

You may want to peruse this book leisurely from cover to cover, picking up ideas for future home projects. Or, if you have a specific task in mind, check the table of contents for the sections of the book that deal with the various aspects of your project. You'll notice that after the brief description of each booklet or packet, there are instructions covering what fee, if any, should be included, the exact title you should ask for (and, in some cases, publication number), and the mailing address. If you have suggestions or encounter problems receiving your "free thing," please write to us: *Free Things for Homeowners*, c/o Cornerstone Library, Simon and Schuster, 1230 Avenue of the Americas, New York, N.Y. 10020.

All of the companies and agencies listed here have agreed to make their publications available through 1981, but due to increased demand, supplies may run out. Also, many government publications are obtainable from more than one agency. For example, a pamphlet published by the Department of Agriculture might be available from the Department's regional office, the Superintendent of Documents in Washington, D.C., the Consumer Information Center in Pueblo, Colorado, or even from your Congressman. One office may have a budget to allow free distribution of the pamphlet; others may not and may request a small handling fee or postage.

We want especially to thank Cornell University, the National Planning Service, and the United States Government for allowing us to list a substantial number of their publications. We also extend our sincere appreciation to the public relations personnel of the many companies and industries whose cooperation greatly assisted our efforts. We hope you enjoy using *Free Things for Homeowners*.

Buying, Building, and Renting

Home Buying

A home is the single largest investment for many people. "Wise Home Buying" is a guide for the prospective buyer with reminders of all the important features to watch for when buying a house. Included is a glossary of critical terms.

Send: a postcard
Ask for: "Wise Home Buying" (HUD-267-H9)
Write to: Superintendent of Documents
U.S. Government Printing Office
Washington, D.C. 20402

Housing Market

The basic considerations for anyone looking for a place to live can be found in "The Housing Market: A Guide to Sensible Choices." Should you rent or buy? How good an investment is a house? What choices are there in terms of you, your family, your values, your finances? Tables and worksheets will help you make your decision.

Send: $1.25
Ask for: "The Housing Market : A Guide to Sensible Choices" (NE-196)
Write to: Distribution Center, Dept. FHO
7 Research Park
Cornell University
Ithaca, N.Y.14850

Shopping for a Home

Choosing and financing a home is usually the biggest financial undertaking in the life of a family. A 24-page brochure, "Selecting and Financing a Home," aims to help you make decisions on renting vs. buying, and offers guidelines on how much you can afford on housing and related costs. Find helpful suggestions for evaluating locations, neighborhoods, and mortgage loans.

Send: $1.50
Ask for: "Selecting and Financing a Home" (147H)
Write to: Superintendent of Documents
U.S. Government Printing Office
Washington, D.C. 20402

Home Buyer's Guide

A 32-page booklet from the National Association of Home Builders, "Home Buyer's Guide" helps you make the best decision possible when it comes to buying a home. Topics range from how much you can afford to pay for a house, to how big your down payment and monthly costs should be. New houses are compared with old and a handy checklist is provided, as well as information on builders, neighborhoods, financing, closing costs, inspections, and tax benefits.

Send: $1.00
Ask for: "Home Buyer's Guide"
Write to: National Association of
Home Builders
15th and M Sts., N.W.
Washington, D.C. 20005

Selecting and financing a home

Analyzing your housing needs: Consider the needs and wants of your family. Set some priorities before you look for a place to live. This is important because the "just right" place is seldom found. It usually is necessary to make some concessions to find a home that suits your family and budget.

Tips for Veterans

The Veterans' Administration has prepared a 38-page guide, "The Home-Buying Veteran," for veterans planning to buy or build homes with a GI loan. This booklet provides comprehensive information on the selection of the right neighborhood, house or lot, describes the general characteristics of property, and discusses both initial costs and possible future

expenses in connection with home ownership. Learn about sales contracts, repayment of loans, and what the VA can and cannot do for the home purchaser.

Send: a postcard
Ask for: "The Home-Buying Veteran" (#26-6)
Write to: Consumer Information Center
Department Z
Pueblo, Colo. 81009

Moving

America is on the go. Statistics say that the average American moves every five years. If you're about to pack up your household, a handy 8-page booklet, "When You Move—Do's and Don'ts," helps you hire a mover and organize your moving day.

Send: a postcard
Ask for: "When You Move—Do's and Don'ts"
Write to: Consumer Information Center
Department Z
Pueblo, Colo. 81009

Buying a Condominium

The advantages and disadvantages of condominium ownership are analyzed and compared in "Condominium Buyer's Guide," 31 pages including a close-up look at what "maintenance" may or may not mean, and the merits of condominium buying as an investment. This booklet covers both new construction and co-op conversion and contains a glossary of condominium terminology.

Send: $1.00
Ask for: "Condominium Buyer's Guide"
Write to: National Association of
Home Builders
15th and M Sts., N.W.
Washington, D.C. 20005

Condominium buyers guide

You will note three basic areas that distinguish between the ownership of a condominium dwelling and the ownership of, say, a single-family house:

The condominium dweller is sole owner of only the inner living space.

. . . all condominium owners jointly owned the grounds and exterior facilities . . .

. . . the condominium owner contributes a monthly fee for the upkeep of the jointly own "common elements."

Cooperatives

As valuable supplies of natural resources dwindle, sharing will come to play a larger part in everyone's life, even in housing. "Advising People About Cooperatives" is a source book for all the various aspects of co-op settlements. This book includes a listing in both periodical and audiovisual form.

Send: 45¢
Ask for: "Advising People About Cooperatives" (PA-1147)
Write to: Superintendent of Documents
U.S. Government Printing Office
Washington, D.C. 20402

Condominiums

An increasing number of prospective homeowners are turning to condominiums to fill their housing needs. The ability to own your own home, plus a share in recreational facilities and other benefits, is very attractive to many investors. "Questions About Condomin-

iums" discusses the benefits and pitfalls of condominium owning, as well as organization concepts, rights and responsibilities. Included are a glossary of terms and a list of HUD regions and area offices.

Send: a postcard
Ask for: "Questions About Condominiums" (HUD-365-H7)
Write to: U.S. Department of Housing and Urban Development
Washington, D.C. 20410

Coops and Condos

Cooperatives and condominiums are the latest development in housing. If you are tired of renting and don't want the responsibility of single-family-home upkeep, perhaps you should look into this new way to own your own home without many of the hassles of property ownership. "Cooperative Housing and Condominiums: Home Ownership with a Difference" will explain the differences.

Send: $1.25
Ask for: "Cooperative Housing and Condominiums: Home Ownership with a Difference" (NE-200)
Write to: Distribution Center, Dept FHO
7 Research Park
Cornell University
Ithaca, N.Y. 14850

Building Jargon

Building your home might turn out to be easier than understanding the vocabulary. The "Homeowner's Glossary of Building Terms" is a "Berlitz handbook" for prospective homeowners entering new territory.

Send: a postcard
Ask for: "Homeowner's Glossary of Building Terms" (HUD-369-H6)
Write to: U.S. Dept. of Housing and Urban Development 451 Seventh St., S.W. Washington, D.C. 20410

Homeowner's glossary of building terms

Batt: Insulation in the form of a blanket, rather than loose filling.
Batten: Small thin strips covering joints between wider boards on exterior building surfaces.

Construction Costs

If you want to build your own home, but rising costs are making it next to impossible, "Home Construction—How to Reduce Costs" can help make your dream a reality. This 16-page booklet shows how major factors in building a house, such as location, design, selection of materials, and construction can radically lower total costs while upholding standards of quality.

Send: 80¢
Ask for: "Home Construction— How to Reduce Costs" (#168)

Write to: Superintendent of Documents U.S. Government Printing Office Washington, D.C. 20402

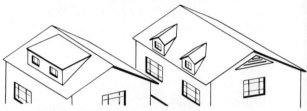

Shed dormers provide more usable space than the gable type.

House construction: how to reduce costs

Economical construction does not mean inferior construction. Poor workmanship and shoddy materials are not economical in the long run. Maintenance and repair costs could soon nullify any initial savings.

House Building—Do It Yourself

From the U.S. Department of Housing and Urban Development comes a manual which demonstrates the basic methods and techniques used in building a home. "How to Build a House Using Self-Help Housing Techniques" is a 50-page booklet employing pictures to teach these skills, and is printed both in English and Spanish.

Send: $1.40
Ask for: "How to Build a House Using Self-Help Housing Techniques" (HUD-345-1A)
Write to: Superintendent of Documents U.S. Government Printing Office Washington, D.C. 20402

Construction

Are you thinking of designing your own home, but you know nothing about it? Here are 64 pages of plans for new homes. Detailed specifications are given for the quality materials used, the pre-assembled building system itself is described, and building estimates are provided to help you save on materials, time and money. A new way to build the home you want at a price already estimated for you.

Send: 25¢
Ask for: "Aladdin Readi-cut Houses"
Write to: The Aladdin Co.
Bay City, Mich. 48706

Pre-fab Homes

Although the idea of building a home in one place and shipping it to another is not a new one, manufactured housing did not come into its own until the last 30 years. Major improvements in materials, construction techniques and quality control made it an attractive alternative to conventionally built homes. A 16-page booklet, "Continental Homes, Here Today, Home Tomorrow," gives you a good look at some of the reasons (besides speed and cost) for selecting manufactured housing.

Send: $1.00
Ask for: "Continental Homes, Here Today,
Home Tomorrow"
Write to: Continental Homes of
New England
Daniel Webster Hwy. South
Nashua, N.H. 03060

Home Designs

The Home Building Plan Service has three new house-plan books complete with architectural floorplans and descriptive explanations. Included are traditional and contemporary designs for year-round living, plans for recreational or holiday cottages, and unique yet practical ideas for hillside homes and sloping lots. You can start to dream and plan now with hundreds of these imaginative homes right at your fingertips.

Send: $1.50 each
Ask for: "Homes for the 80's"
"Recreation and Holiday Homes"
"Hillside Homes"
Write to: Home Building Plan Service
2235 N.E. Sandy Blvd.
Portland, Ore. 97232

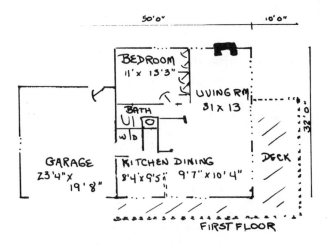

New Homes

A 104-page catalog, "350 New Homes," may be the easiest way ever invented to shop for the home that's right for you. All kinds of houses are represented here; small or spacious, contemporary or traditional, modest or expensive. There's a home here for every taste and pocketbook. When you find the one you like, construction blueprints may be ordered.

Send: $1.50
Ask for: "350 New Homes"
Write to: L.M. Bruinier & Associates Inc.
1304 S.W. Bertha Blvd.
Portland, Ore. 97219

Vacation Homes

Whether you vacation in snowy mountains or on a sandy beach, "Vacation Homes" will give you ideas for your own away-from-it-all home, beautifully trimmed with cedar. Lush photographs of homes in their natural settings reveal how easy it is to design a building that complements the elements of nature—and all with shingles and handsplit shakes.

Send: 35¢
Ask for: "Vacation Homes"
Write to: Red Cedar Shingle and
Handsplit Shake Bureau
515 116th Ave., N.E., Suite 275
Bellevue, Wash. 98004

House Plans

Fantasies are finally realized when people build vacation or weekend homes. "A Portfolio of Leisure Design Homes" illustrates these

first floor

dreams with drawings and architectural plans for over 83 imaginative homes. Find your dream house, whether it be a forest A-frame, a Dutch-colonial country barn, a mountain chalet, or a seaside cottage.

Send: $1.50
Ask for: "A Portfolio of Leisure Design Homes"
Write to: Master Plan Service
89 E. Jericho Tpke.
Mineola, N.Y. 11501

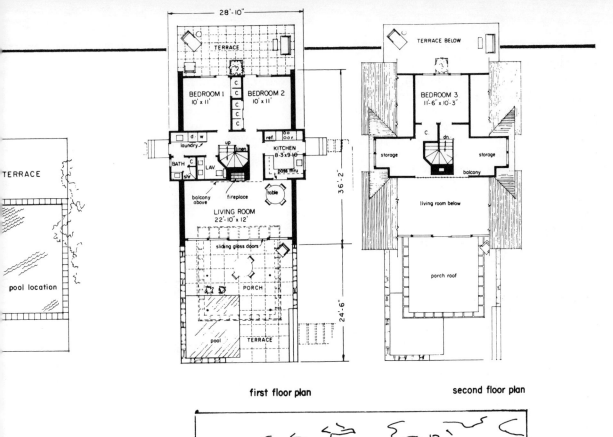

TERRACE

pool location

28'-10"

TERRACE

BEDROOM 1
10' x 11'

BEDROOM 2
10' x 11'

c
c
c
c
c
c

d w laundry

ref. co or

BATH

c

LAV

shr

up

linen

KITCHEN
8'-3 x 9'-10

pass thru

balcony above   fireplace

table

LIVING ROOM
22'-10" x 12'

sliding glass doors

36'-2"

PORCH

pool

TERRACE

24'-6"

first floor plan

TERRACE BELOW

BEDROOM 3
11'-6" x 10'-3"

c

dn

storage

storage

balcony

living room below

porch roof

second floor plan

Housing

A 16-page booklet from the Manufactured Housing Institute, "Housing for the 1980's," explains why economical housing, such as mobile and pre-assembled homes, has become so popular. The demographics of the mobile-home-buying public, as well as energy efficiency, safety, and economy are discussed in question-answer format.

Send: a postcard
Ask for: "Housing for the 1980's"
Write to: Manufactured Housing Institute
1745 Jefferson Davis Hwy.
Suite 511
Arlington, Va. 22202

Housing Designs

"100 Affordable Homes" is a book of house designs. In its 98 pages you'll find homes of all types and sizes, featuring a wide variety of prices. There is a special section on vacation homes and information on ordering full construction blueprints. Here's an opportunity to house-hunt without leaving home!

Send: $1.50
Ask for: "100 Affordable Homes"
Write to: Homes for Living Inc.
107-40 Queens Blvd.
Forest Hills, N.Y. 11375

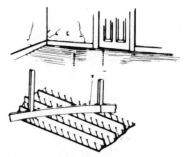

Inspecting the Older House

As the construction industry continues to suffer inflationary setbacks, larger and larger numbers of prospective buyers are turning to older houses. "How to Inspect the Older House" guides you through every aspect of the older home. Simple explanations and diagrams show what to look for in plumbing and electrical systems, beams, basements, and other important areas. Nine pages include a comprehensive home checklist.

Send: $1.00
Ask for: "How to Inspect the Older House" (IB-165)
Write to: Distribution Center, Dept. FHO
7 Research Park
Cornell University
Ithaca, N.Y. 14850

Renovation

As old houses become an endangered species, more and more people are choosing to revitalize them, both for their unique character and beauty, and for past reliability. If you've fallen in love with an old house, check first with "Renovate an Old House" to determine whether a renovation will be worth your time and money. Twenty pages show you how to check basic structure, and where to look for signs of possible decay and damage.

Send: $1.10
Ask for: "Renovate an Old House" (#212)
Write to: Superintendent of Documents
U.S. Government Printing Office
Washington, D.C. 20402

Renovate an old house

The two strength properties that decay reduces are hardness and toughness. Therefore, one way to determine the extent of damage is to prod the wood with a sharp tool to see if it mars easily, or to pry out a splinter to check on toughness. If toughness has been greatly reduced by decay, the wood may break across the grain with little splintering and lift out with little resistance.

House Renovation

For the person who loves old houses, a pamphlet—"Remodeling a House—Will It Be Worthwhile?"—gives sound, clear advice on evaluating the feasibility of remodeling. Information is given on inspecting the frame, sidings, windows, roof, and interior. Also: how to tell if a house has been insulated, has insect damage, decay, or water seepage. And finally —enjoy your new old house!

Send: a postcard
Ask for: "Remodeling a House—Will It Be Worthwhile?" (606H)
Write to: Consumer Information Center
Department Z
Pueblo, Colo. 81009

Remodeling a house: Will it be worth it?

Consider the arrangement of the house and the changes that may be required for convenience. Look at the rooms in terms of furniture placement and adequate circulation space. Also consider storage requirements. Many older homes have few, if any, closets. Do not be bound to traditional uses of rooms, but look at spaces in terms of your living requirements.

Home Rental

In a society that is constantly on the move, many people prefer to rent rather than own their homes. "Wise Rental Practices" details the increasingly complex areas of landlord rights and responsibilities vs. tenant rights and responsibilities, plus advice on how to search for a rental property. Its 39 pages include a complete list of HUD regional and area offices.

Send: a postcard
Ask for: "Wise Rental Practices" (HUD-470-NVACP-2)
Write to: Consumer Information Center
Department Z
Pueblo, Colo. 81009

Renting

Security deposits, subletting, eviction proce-dures, leases, insurance, roommates, tenant organizations, and other thorny problems are discussed in "For Rent: A Consumer's Guide to Rental Housing." Worksheets help you study and evaluate your lease, your budget and your housing values.

Send: $1.25
Ask for: "For Rent: A Consumer's Guide to Rental Housing" (NE-198)
Write to: Distribution Center, Dept. FHO
7 Research Park
Cornell University
Ithaca, N.Y. 14850

Wise rental practices

Looking for a place to live is like looking for employment. It is important to make a good impression on the prospec-tive landlord. Apply in person. Be persistent and cour-teous. Fill out the application form completely and honestly. Leave no blank spaces. If the landlord is not accepting applications, ask if there is a waiting list.

General Home Maintenance

Combination Square

Carpentry Projects

"Home Projects You Can Build," a 50-page booklet from *Better Home and Gardens*, contains all-time-best home carpentry projects you can send for with 114 tested plans for building with professional results. Projects include storage containers, planters, bunkbed units, playhouses, and homemade furniture and toys.

Send: $1.25

Ask for: "Home Projects You Can Build"

Write to: National Plan Service
435 W. Fullerton Ave.
Elmhurst, Ill. 60126

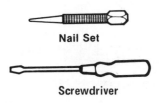

Nail Set

Screwdriver

BASIC HAND TOOLS

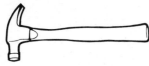

Claw Hammer

Hand Saw

Home projects you can build

Basic Woodworking Tools

You don't need a complete set of fancy woodworking tools to build projects for your home—not even for most of the extensive built-ins described and listed in this book. A set of basic hand tools will do the job.

Home Improvement

A series of notebook-page brochures, "The *Family Handyman* Information Bank" is a positive wealth of home improvement information: ways to cut heat loss, a guide to home energy product rip-offs, how to select a wood-burning stove, how to handle water damage or open plugged drains, how to build a wine rack. All this and much more!

Send: $1.50

Ask for: "The *Family Handyman* Information Bank"

Write to: *Family Handyman* Magazine
1999 Shepard Rd.
St. Paul, Minn. 55116

Insulating basement walls

Frame a 2x4 wall adjacent to the concrete wall. Set studs 16″ o.c.; secure to floor with concrete nails.

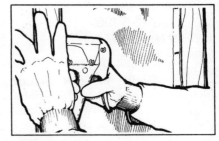

Install the batts so the vapor barrier faces toward the heated side of the wall. Staple flanges tightly to 2x4s.

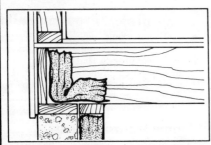

Fold batts as shown to insulate along the band joists. This area is often neglected, results in heat loss.

Install wallboard or paneling over the insulation. Heat loss through uninsulated basement walls can be 20%.

Plumbing

Sinks, sewers, pipes, drains, faucets and toilets are less mysterious and less messy if you know how they work. "Plumbing Repairs" will give you the terminology, tools and techniques to keep your pipelines flowing. You'll learn how to unclog toilets, install faucets, fix drips and prevent future problems.

Send: $1.25
Ask for: "Plumbing Repairs"
Write to: National Plan Service
435 W. Fullerton Ave.
Elmhurst, Ill. 60126

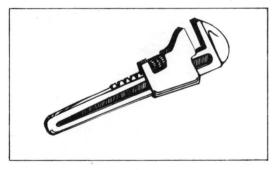

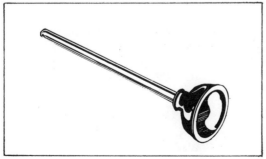

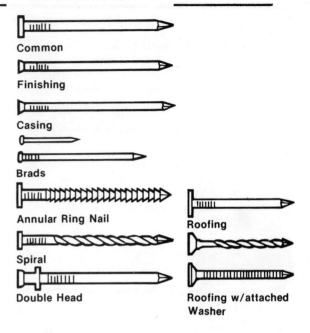

Common

Finishing

Casing

Brads

Annular Ring Nail

Spiral

Double Head

Roofing

Roofing w/attached Washer

Carpentry

"Basic Home Carpentry" is a 50-page manual that will give you a crash course on all the basics. You'll learn how to organize your workshop, select nails and screws, identify the various parts of power tools and use them correctly. This illustrated guidebook will even give you decorator ideas for things you can make with a simple box. And much more.

Send: $1.25
Ask for: "Basic Home Carpentry"
Write to: National Plan Service
435 W. Fullerton Ave.
Elmhurst, Ill. 60126

Home Repairs

"The Hyde Tool House How-To Guide" will show how to check your house for maintenance, remodeling or restoration. You'll learn that you can do simple jobs with simple tools if you have these helpful hints and tips. You don't need to call in professionals for jobs you can do.

Send: $1.00

Ask for: "The Hyde Tool House How-To Guide"

Write to: Hyde Manufacturing Co. Southbridge, Mass. 01550

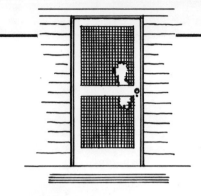

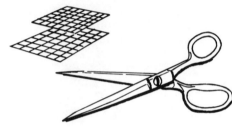

Inside Repairs

Leaking faucets, loose tiles, squeaking doors, and cracks in the walls not only nag at you persistently, but lead to further damage and deterioration in your home. "Simple Home Repairs—inside" is a 23-page booklet designed to make repair jobs just that—simple. Common indoor problems are defined, necessary tools are listed, and how-to steps for fixing are carefully outlined and illustrated.

Send: $1.50

Ask for: "Simple Home Repairs—inside"

Write to: Superintendent of Documents U.S. Government Printing Office Washington, D.C. 20402

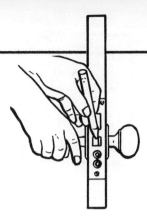

Superior interiors: red cedar shingle and handsplit shake

Apply your shingles or shakes to the nailing strips. Start at the bottom, putting two nails or staples into each shingle or shake where it overlaps the second nailing strip from the floor. Apply second row so that shingles or shakes just cover the first row of nail heads. Continue in this manner to the top row.

Simple home repairs . . . inside

How-to turn off water:
First turn off the water at the shut-off valve nearest to the faucet you are going to repair. Then turn on the faucet until the water stops flowing.

Red Cedar Interiors

The 8-page "Superior Interiors" shows some of the beautiful and exciting ideas you can employ to decorate with cedar shakes and shingles. Besides perking up your house, cedar shingles and shakes are practical—they retain their beauty with little or no maintenance. A good, short do-it-yourself section concludes this handsome booklet.

Send: 35¢
Ask for: "Superior Interiors"
Write to: Red Cedar Shingle & Handsplit Shake Bureau 515 116th Ave., N.E., Suite 275 Bellevue, Wash. 98004

Indoor Cedar Projects

Cedar shingles are beautiful indoors, too. Plus, they smell good. A booklet, "How to Do It and Save With Economy-Grade Red Cedar Shakes and Shingles," gives you lots of handsome ideas for indoor decorating with cedar.

Send: 10¢
Ask for: "How To Do It and Save With Economy-Grade Red Cedar Shakes and Shingles"
Write to: Red Cedar Shingle & Handsplit Shake Bureau
515 116th Ave., N.E., Suite 275
Bellevue, Wash. 98004

Electric Wiring

Complicated wiring is best left to a professional, but some simple procedures can be undertaken by the homeowner. "Electrical Wiring Basics" helps you to better understand and manage the electrical system in your home, with 50 pages on wiring and installation instructions and diagrams, as well as grounding procedures.

Send: $1.25
Ask for: "Electrical Wiring Basics"
Write to National Plan Service
435 W. Fullerton Ave.
Elmhurst, Ill. 60126

House Cleaning

If you love a clean and tidy house, but a full-time job or small children make this next to impossible, consult "Basics of Housecleaning and Home Care." This 21-page booklet gets down to the really nitty "gritty" of housework by helping organize cleaning time and outlining basic cleaning procedures for every surface in the home.

Send: 30¢
Ask for: "Basics of Housecleaning and Home Care" (IB-69)
Write to: Distribution Center, Dept. FHO
7 Research Park
Cornell University
Ithaca, N.Y. 14853

Walls, Floors, and Ceilings

Remodeling

What are houses made of? "Floors, Walls, and Ceilings"! Most of our home-remodeling projects will center on these areas. This 52-page how-to guide helps you choose and construct 12 different floors, 9 different walls, and 7 different ceilings. Also included: windows, doors, dormers, and skylights.

Send: $1.25
Ask for: "Floors, Walls, and Ceilings"
Write to: National Plan Service
435 W. Fullerton Ave.
Elmhurst, Ill. 60126

Floors, walls, and ceilings

If you're tackling a flooring project, read the entire chapter on flooring, rather than just the section pertaining to the type of floor you're installing. Many techniques apply across the board, and you'll find yourself borrowing ideas from several related sections.

Interior Decorating

When you have a room you want to redecorate and you don't know where to begin, ask Armstrong for ideas to perk up your floors, ceilings, and walls. Ask for information on whatever job you plan to tackle and receive Armstrong pamphlets and literature to get you started.

Send: a postcard
Ask for: "Armstrong Pamphlets"
Write to: Armstrong World Industries
Box 3001
Lancaster, Pa. 17604

Armstrong pamphlets

. . . small samples of fabrics, paints, and other materials can help you and your retailer select a flooring design that will harmonize with the existing colors in any rooms adjacent to the one in which your new floor will be installed.

Walls and Ceilings

For the do-it-yourselfer, Georgia-Pacific has 3 handy booklets for the care of walls and ceilings. Whether you want to construct a wall with gypsum wallboard, whether you need to repair and patch your old wall, or whether you just want to give your old wall a new texture, these simple, direct pamphlets will pave the way.

Send: a postcard
Ask for: "Wall and Ceiling Texturing"
          "Wall Repairing and Patching"
          "Gypsum Wallboard Application"
Write to: Georgia-Pacific
          900 S.W. Fifth Ave.
          Portland, Ore. 97204

Redoing Walls

"Painting and Wallpapering," a 52-page booklet from *Better Homes and Gardens*, is a guide with emphasis on the care and use of tools for these home projects. Both exterior and interior surfaces of the home are analyzed and discussed in terms of preparation and finishing when painting or wallpapering.

Send: $1.25
Ask for: "Painting and Wallpapering"
Write to: National Plan Service
          435 W. Fullerton Ave.
          Elmhurst, Ill. 60126

PAINTING MASONRY

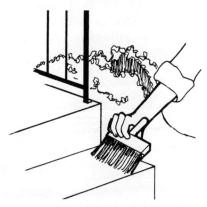

The pock marks in masonry soak up paint like a sponge. The best tool to use is a stiff-bristled brush.

COMMON BRUSH HANDLES

Beavertail   Pencil   Kaiser   Flat

The four common handle styles for paint brushes are the beavertail, the pencil, the kaiser, and the flat. Each has a definite function. The beavertail handle is found on the wide brushes and is easy to grip. The pencil and flat handles allow greater fingertip control. The kaiser handle offers the control of the pencil and flat handles with an easy-to-hold grip.

Painting and wallpapering

Rollers, like brushes, leave lap marks—especially when you try to spread paint with a full roller. Crisscross your strokes while you're putting on both the first and second coats. The crossing action will cancel the lap marks.

Wallcoverings

Walls don't have to be covered with paint or paper. There are other, natural materials, such as grass, cork, bamboo and foliage, that can beautify a dull room. A handy packet from Shibui contains over 70 samples and preliminary instructions for using out-of-doors materials inside the house.

Send: $2.00 (deductible from first order)
Ask for: "Shibui Wallcoverings Kit"
Write to: Shibui Wallcoverings
Box 1638
Rohnert Park, Calif. 94928

Wallcoverings

Practical how-to information is packed into "All You Need to Know About Wallcoverings." This 16-page booklet begins with sensible decorating hints, then helps you analyze the type of wallcovering that best suits your needs,

teaches you to measure accurately before you buy, and then lists all the tools and equipment you'll need to do the kind of job you'll be proud of.

Send: 50¢

Ask for: 'All You Need to Know About Wallcoverings"

Write to: The Wallcovering
Information Bureau
66 Morris Ave.
Springfield, N.J. 07081

All you need to know about wall–coverings

In planning the decoration of a room, keep in mind your preferences. Asking too many opinions of friends will only confuse you. It's your taste and imagination that gives your rooms the character that makes them different from those of your neighbor.

Paneling a Room

This fold-out poster, "How to Panel a Room," gives you a guide you can put on the wall and follow as you work. All the separate steps for a perfectly paneled wall right before your eyes —necessary tools, measurements, grain matching, cutting window openings, caulking, finishing with mouldings.

Send: $1.50

Ask for: "How to Panel a Room"

Write to: Masonite Corp.
29 N. Wacker Dr.
Chicago, Ill. 60606

How to panel a room

Step number one is to measure the length, width and height of the area to be paneled. Then draw an outline plan of the area showing the overall dimensions.

Wall Paneling

There's no mystery to installing wall paneling if you know what you're doing. This 26-page booklet, beautifully photographed and illustrated to help you understand what you need to do at each stage of your project, will let you panel any room with ease. There are even sections on unusual architecture and troublesome construction and arches and alcoves.

Send: $1.00

Ask for: "The Paneling Book"

Write to: Georgia-Pacific
900 S.W. Fifth Ave.
Portland, Ore. 97204

Paneling Designs

Not all paneled walls look alike. Almost any look you want to achieve is possible—formal English oak, rustic "used" red brick, white French provincial, weathered barn siding, knotty pine, patterns and florals, woods of all colors and textures. "Paneling Ideas" can add immediate value to your home.

Send: $1.50
Ask for: "Paneling Ideas"
Write to: Masonite Corp.
29 N. Wacker Dr.
Chicago, Ill. 60606

Wall Paneling

When you get tired of looking at the same four walls, remember that you can turn them into one or more new walls with attractive paneling. Even if you're not a carpenter, "Instructions for Installing Wall Paneling" will show you how to give your room that professional look. Measurement, sawing, nailing, gluing and year-round care for your paneled walls are easy to learn with this handy instruction manual.

Send: a postcard
Ask for: "Instructions for Installing Wall Paneling"
Write to: Weyerhaeuser
Box 1188
Chesapeake, Va. 23320

Wood Mouldings

Want to know the history of wood mouldings? Are you curious about how mouldings are

Write to: Wood Moulding and
Millwork Producers
Box 25278
Portland, Ore. 97225

manufactured? Are you worried about depleting our forests? A 48-page booklet, "From Tree to Trim," will inform you on all this and teach you how to buy, measure, install, and finish mouldings and jambs.

Send: $1.50
Ask for: "From Tree to Trim"
Write to: Western Wood Moulding
and Millwork Producers
Box 25278
Portland, Ore. 97225

Wood Moulding Ideas

If you need ideas on how to spruce up a drab room, consider "Design and Decorate with Wood Mouldings." This beautifully photographed and illustrated 8-page pamphlet will introduce you to the beauty of wood that can trim and transform your room into its own special look.

Send: 75¢
Ask for: "Design and Decorate with Wood Mouldings"

Colonial Wood Mouldings

Whether you live in an 18th-century house or not, you may want to beautify your home with colonial wood mouldings. "American Colonial" will show you how to create authentic room mouldings for ceilings, wall panels, chair rails, baseboards, and exterior trim for doors and windows from materials available at your local building materials store.

Send: 60¢
Ask for: "American Colonial"

Write to: Wood Moulding and
Millwork Producers
Box 25278
Portland, Ore. 97225

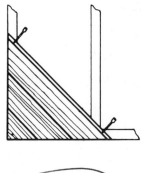

Wood Moulding

Once you've decided on wood mouldings for your home, "How to Work with Wood Mouldings" will give you step-by-step procedures for actually installing them. This 15-page illustrated manual will teach you everything from measuring your room to putting over the last nail.

Send: 50¢
Ask for: "How to Work with
Wood Mouldings"
Write to: Western Moulding and
Millwork Producers
Box 25278
Portland, Ore. 97225

Redwood Paneling

"Redwood Construction Tips—Panel a Room with Redwood Lumber" is a handy, informative folder from the California Redwood Association, designed to help you beautify your walls. Instructions include vertical, horizontal, and diagonal paneling, as well as tips for mouldings, baseboards, and electrical outlets.

Send: 35¢
Ask for: "Redwood Construction Tips—
Panel a Room"
Write to: California Redwood Association
One Lombard St.
San Francisco, Calif. 94111

Paneling

Don't get stuck up just because paneling a room looks so easy. H.B. Fuller will help you plan a room paneling job carefully *before* they provide you with the glue. Their instruction booklet, "How to Panel a Room Without Climbing the Walls," also includes a handy materials checklist.

Send: 35¢
Ask for: "How to Panel a Room Without Climbing the Walls"
Write to: H.B. Fuller Co.
Construction and Consumer Products Division
315 Shuth Hicks Rd.
Palatine, Ill. 60067

Trimming a Room

Mouldings have always been a mark of fine building. "The Collection by Focal Point, Inc." focuses on moulding patterns, as well as ceiling medallions, mantles, domes, overdoor pieces, stair brackets, and more. The 12-page booklet includes photographs, measurements, and installation information.

Send: $1.50
Ask for: "The Collection by Focal Point, Inc."
Write to: Focal Point, Inc.
2005 Marietta Rd., N.W.
Atlanta, Ga. 30318

Rugs

A 14-page booklet from Bissel, "Guide to Complete Carpet Care," is designed to provide you with the simple steps necessary to ensure the beauty and life of your carpet. Includes spot and stain removal methods, beauty tips, and facts on fiber construction.

Send: a postcard
Ask for: "Guide to Complete Carpet Care"
Write to: Bissel Inc.
Consumer Service Institute
Grand Rapids, Mich. 49501

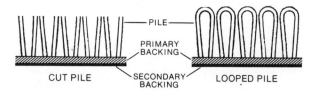

Rugs

If you can have but one furnishing, make it a rug! Rugs insulate and cushion floors, reduce noise, and add warmth, color, and elegance to a room. A 31-page booklet, "The Selection of Rugs and Carpets," ends confusion about what kind of rug to buy, and how to maintain it. A handy fiber chart tells you about rug construction, resistance to abrasion and soil, and resiliency.

Send: 65¢

Ask for: "The Selection of Rugs and
Carpets" (NE-192)

Write to: Distribution Center, Dept. FHO
Cornell University
7 Research Park
Ithaca, N.Y. 14850

Tile Floors

A complete kit on floor tiles is "Kentile's Fashions in Floors." Besides a full-color brochure on dozens of floor tiles, this handy set includes an 8-page booklet on installing tile floors. Learn how to prepare the underfloor, lay out the room, spread the adhesive, lay the tile, install wallbase, etc.

Send: 75¢

Ask for: "Kentile Fashions in Floors"

Write to: Kentile Floors
58 Second Ave.
Brooklyn, N.Y. 11215

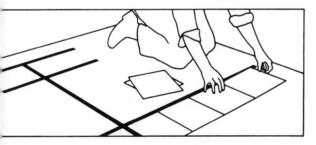

How to install your own your own Kentile floors

Fitting tile around door jambs . . . Perhaps the neatest way of all is to make a simple saw cut at the base of the door frame. Remember, the door jamb is not a structural support and you can easily take a carpenter's saw and make a quick saw cut to remove about ⅛″ of the frame at the base.

Hardwood Flooring

Oak flooring carrying the NOFMA trademark is a precision-made product of enduring beauty. But for the ultimate in appearance and performance the installer must pay close attention to a number of details both before and during the installation process. An 8-page "Hardware Flooring Installation Manual" describes the simplest methods of achieving successful installations with various types of oak (and other hardwood) flooring. Information on handling and storage of flooring materials is also included.

Send: 50¢

Ask for: "Hardwood Flooring
Installation Manual"

Write to: National Oak Flooring
Manufacturing Assn.
804 Sterick Bldg.
Memphis, Tenn. 38103

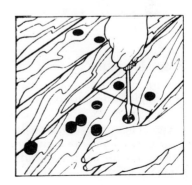

Hardwood flooring installation manual

Laying a new strip floor over an old floor:
The existing wood floor can serve as a sub-floor. Drive down any raised nails, renail loose boards and replace any warped boards that can't be made level. Sweep and clean the floor well, but don't use water.

Remove thresholds to allow the new flooring to run flush through doorways, remove doors and baseboard. Lay building paper over the old floor.

Always install the new floor at right angles to the old floor boards.

Maple Flooring

"Spec-Data" offers very practical, thorough, and helpful information about maple flooring: the various grades of materials and their various uses. You'll learn how to determine the number of feet of flooring you need and which finishes work best.

Send: a postcard
Ask for: "Spec-Data"
Write to: Maple Flooring Manufacturers
Association Inc.
2400 East Devon Ave.
Des Plaines, Ill. 60018

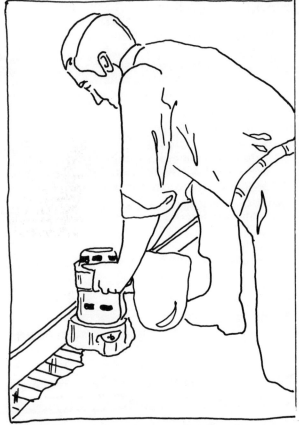

Wood Floor Finishes

For solid information on transforming your old floors into glowing 'new' ones, check with "How to Finish Wood Floors . . . Old or New." This 8-page brochure begins with surface preparation of the old floor (including detailed instructions for sanding), moves on to staining, filling nail holes and final finishing.

Quick help for tired floors!
Send: 50¢
Ask for: "How to Finish Wood Floors . . . Old or New"
Write to: Pierce and Stevens Chemical Corp.
P.O. Box 1092
Buffalo, N.Y. 14240

Installing Hardwood Floors

If you have soiled or worn-out floors, you could install your own new hardwood floor if you follow the steps in "How to Install Williamsburg Strip Prefinished Hardwood Flooring." This handy little pamphlet will show you how to get your room ready, check your subfloor, use a powernailer, and lay the field of your floor from the "starter" wall right up that far wall. You'll learn the tricks the pros use.

Send: 25¢

Ask for: "How to Install Williamsburg Strip Prefinished Hardwood Flooring"

Write to: Memphis Hardwood
Flooring Company
Box 7253
Memphis, Tenn. 38107

Wood Flooring

Like fine furniture, oak (and other hardwood) flooring needs proper finishing to enhance its grain and color and to protect it against wear and abuse. Poor quality or poorly applied finish allows the wood's natural beauty to deteriorate and creates an unnecessary maintenance problem. An 8-page manual, "Hardwood Flooring Finishing/Refinishing Manual," describes the methods and products which will produce a beautiful, lasting finish for fine wood flooring and restore beauty even to worn and neglected older hardwood floors.

Send: 50¢

Ask for: "Hardwood Flooring Finishing/Refinishing Manual"

Write to: National Oak Flooring
Manufacturers Association
804 Sterick Bldg.
Memphis, Tenn. 38103

Hardwood flooring finishing/refinishing manual

In this manual we have incorporated many years of research and practical experience to describe the methods and products that will give a beautiful, lasting finish to oak and other hardwood flooring, and to restore the beauty to old hardwood floors that have become unsightly from wear or neglect.

Furniture, Appliances, and Accessories

Furniture Care

Before you throw out old furniture, send for "Repairing and Refinishing Furniture" from the "*Better Homes and Gardens* Guide-to" Series. This 52-page booklet demonstrates the use of tools and materials for furniture repair, refinishing, and painting. Extra: instructions for specialty finishes.

Send: $1.25
Ask for: "Repairing and Refinishing Furniture"
Write to: National Plan Service
435 W. Fullerton Ave.
Elmhurst, Ill. 60126

Furniture—repairing and refinishing

A really old and dirty piece of furniture may actually have a good finish. So, your first step is to wash it thoroughly with a mixture of soap, water, boiled linseed oil, and alcohol. Rub the surfaces briskly, a small spot at a time, until the cloth drags. Wash a second time with soap and water, then rinse with clear water.

Cast-Iron Furniture

Revisit the traditional Old South with "A Return to Elegance," a catalog from the Moultrie Co. Thirty pages of cast-metal reproductions of settees, tree benches, fountains, gazebos, and more—straight out of another era. Extra: fold-outs of gate designs and driveway entrance kits.

Send: $1.00
Ask for: "A Return to Elegance"
Write to: Moultrie Manufacturing Company
Moultrie, Ga. 31768

A return to elegance

It seems our ancestors still live, here in the Deep South . . .
At times, as we stand surrounded by the legacy of history
in the masterpieces we produce, watching proud crafts-
men turn out creations of ageless grace and beauty, we
experience a sense of wonder. Not that we seem to have
travelled back in time—nobody really wants to do that,
anyway. But now and then, time seems to stop. It's as
though our ancestors are watching.

Furniture Care

Furniture Care Prescription: Take three parts
each: precaution, routine cleaning, and special attention. Then follow directions in "Recipe for Furniture Care." Its 22 pages include
precautionary ingredients, cleaning menus,
and à la carte tips for surfaces. Includes uphol-
stery.
Send: 50¢ plus stamped self-addressed envelope
Ask for: "Recipe for Furniture Care"
Write to: National Association of Furniture
Manufacturers
840l Connecticut Ave., Suite 911
Washington, D.C. 20015

Recipe for furniture care

Spot clean method for grease and oil-based stains:
Dampen a small absorbent cloth with dry-cleaning sol-
vent, or spot remover. Apply carefully to spot from outer
edge to center. Pat and blot with another clean, dry cloth.
Repeat several times as necessary, turning cloths, so stain
doesn't redeposit on fabric.

Leather Chairs

For a catalog on hand-crafted leather chairs,
send for "Leather Chairs." This booklet fea-
tures 32 originals and reproductions of fa-
mous leather chairs, including the
Continental, the Saddle, El Presidente, the
Bauhaus chair, and the director's chair. Extra
Bonus: free leather samples!
Send: $1.00
Ask for: "Leather Chairs"
Write to: Leather Crafter
303 E. 51st St.
New York, N.Y. 10022

Furniture

One of America's best-known furniture authorities has created a number of products designed to give you the furniture finishes you want, safely and in an almost foolproof fashion, but without stripping away the patina or the rich color which adds so much to the character of wood. He also has products and suggestions for dealing with unfinished furniture.

Send: a postcard
Ask for: "Homer Formby's Furniture Fact Book"
Write to: Formby's, Inc.
P.O. Box 667
Olive Branch, Miss. 38654

Butcher Blocks

For a handsome little booklet from the people who first introduced butcher-block furniture, send for the J&D Brauner Butcher Block catalog. Here is butcher block at its best—49 pages

of tables, chairs, chopping blocks, etc., in America's new wood fashion craze.

Send: $1.00
Ask for: "J&D Brauner Butcher Block"
Write to: J&D Brauner Butcher Block
316 E. 59th St.
New York, N.Y. 10022

Old-fashioned Curtains

For an old-fashioned curtain catalog complete with sample swatches for every item featured, send for "Old Manor House." This catalog features curtains derived from early Maryland, Virginia and Pennsylvania homes. Twenty pages include guides to help you measure windows and find curtain styles.

Send: $1.00
Ask for: "Old Manor House"
Write to: Mather's
31-32 E. Main St.
Westminster, Md. 21157

Furniture Catalogs

The "Cohasset Colonials by Hagerty" catalog of furniture kits displays Colonial chairs, Shaker tables, four-poster beds, Coffin clocks,

Wood turner

hutch cabinets, school benches and other treasures from the Early American household. If that's not enough, how about pewter bowls, candlestick lamps, brass door knockers, Colonial fabric and a short course on staining?

Send: $1.00
Ask for: "Cohasset Colonials—Furniture Kits for Home Assembly Catalog"
Write to: Cohasset Colonials
Cohasset, Mass. 02025

Metal Furniture

Clean furniture lasts longer and discourages insects and disease. For simple instructions on cleaning metal furniture, send for "Cleaning Metal Furniture," an illustrated instruction sheet.

Send: 35¢
Ask for: "Cleaning Metal Furniture" (PA-1070)
Write to: Superintendent of Documents
U.S. Government Printing Office
Washington, D.C. 20402

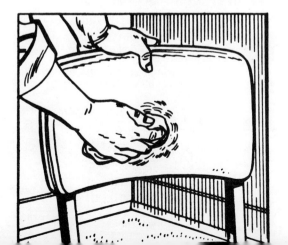

Used Appliances

A used appliance can be a lifesaver for the strained family budget, yet there are pitfalls to be avoided. "Buying a Used Appliance" is a leaflet taking you through the used appliance market. Seven pages warn you what to watch out for, which questions to ask, and what points to consider when buying refrigerators, freezers, washers, dryers, ranges, etc.

Send: $1.00
Ask for: "Buying a Used Appliance" (#1102)
Write to: Publications Division
Office of Governmental and
Public Affairs
U.S. Department of Agriculture
Washington, D.C. 20250

Buying a used appliance

Before shopping for a used appliance, look over the new models. Get acquainted with new features and cost. Compare features on the less expensive models with those on more expensive models. This will help you judge whether the price of the used equipment is reasonable.

Home Freezers

When shopping every day for fresh foods becomes inconvenient and even impossible, the solution is freezing. The 48-page "Freezer Book" helps you save and freeze food efficiently and safely, while preserving its natural color, flavor, and nutritive quality. It shows the correct methods of preparing and packaging every kind of food for freezing, be it shrimp, stringbeans, or spaghetti. Also: keeping freezing charts, guarding against spoilage, even recipes for preparing frozen foods.

Send: 75¢
Ask for: "Freezer Book"
Write to: Ball Corporation
 Muncie, Ind. 47302

Freezer Book

THESE DO NOT FREEZE WELL:
 cake icings
 made with egg whites,
 cream fillings,
 fruit jelly in sandwiches,
 mayonnaise,
 meringue.

Appliance Repairs

Have you ever called a repairman in to fix a broken appliance, only to discover you forgot to plug it in? Statistics say that 40% of all service calls are unnecessary, or deal with minor, easily correctable problems. "How to Avoid Unnecessary Service Calls on Your Electric Appliances" helps you distinguish between real and minor problems with your range, refrigerator, dishwasher, washing machine, air conditioner, etc. A handy 24-page checklist covers common household appliances, typical possible operating problems, the causes, and easy solutions you employ yourself to avoid costly service bills and wasted time waiting for the repairman.

Send: a postcard
Ask for: "How to Avoid Unnecessary Service
 Calls on Your Electric Appliances"
Write to: Edison Electric Institute
 1111 19th St., N.W.
 Washington, D.C. 20036

How to avoid unnecessary service calls on your electric appliances

If there is no electric power in the house, see if your neighbors have power. If they don't, report the matter to your electric utility company; if they do, then your main fuse has probably blown. Replace fuse and, if you still do not have power, call your utility for help.

Kitchen Ranges

With today's fast-paced life and two-career families, time saved on cooking, thawing foods, and cleaning ovens is time well spent on something else. "How to Use Your Electric Range for All It's Worth" is a 43-page booklet by Edison Electric designed to help you select and use your range for top performance Charts help synchronize cooking, baking, and roasting with oven temperatures, while recipes make your meals quick and delicious.

Send: a postcard
Ask for: "How to Use Your Electric Range for All It's Worth"
Write to: Edison Electric Institute
1111 19th St., N.W.
Washington, D.C. 20036

How to use your electic range for all its worth

The size and shape of baking pans affect the volume and texture of the baked foods. When using glass reduce oven temperature 25°.

Appliance Labels

How can you determine which appliance will *really* be cheaper in the long run when buying refrigerators, clothes washers, dishwashers, water heaters, and air conditioners? "Appliance Labeling," a fold-out from the U.S. Department of Energy, helps you understand the now mandatory *Energy Guide* label, which computes yearly operation costs, as compared to price of these appliances.

Send: a postcard
Ask for: "Appliance Labeling"
Write to: U.S. Department of Energy
Technical Information Center
P.O. Box 62
Oak Ridge, Tenn. 37830

Kitchen Appliances

"Coffee, tea, or heat?" That's what we'll be asking if dwindling energy reserves force us to make decisions between water heaters, ranges, or refrigerators. Force the three heaviest consumers of household energy to cut down on consumption with tips from "3 and Me," a 12-page booklet from the Edison Electric Institute.

Send: a postcard
Ask for: "3 and Me"
Write to: Edison Electric Institute
1111 19th St., N.W.
Washington, D.C. 20036

Appliances

A handy little 21-page booklet, "Appliance Care Package and How to Buy a New One Too," gets down to the very basics when it comes to buying a new appliance, and caring for the ones you already have. No-nonsense advice includes a safety list for specific appliances.

Send: a postcard
Ask for: "Appliance Care Package and How to Buy a New One Too"
Write to: Whirlpool Corporation
Department of Corporate and Public Affairs
Benton Harbor, Mich. 49022

Send: 25¢
Ask for: "Understanding Automatic Dishwashers" (IB-3)
Write to: Distribution Center, Dept. FHO
7 Research Park
Cornell University
Ithaca, N.Y. 14850

Portable Appliances

While every American owns several small appliances, keeping them all in operating condition can be costly and confusing. "A Consumer's Guide to Portable Appliances"

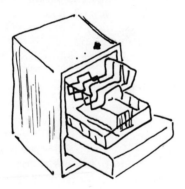

Automatic Dishwashers

A dishwasher saves you hours of work, but it's yet another household machine to operate and cope with. "Understanding Automatic Dishwashers" will help you choose the right machine and keep it running efficiently so it can take over and do the rest!

strives to simplify portable appliance ownership by first asking, "Who needs this?" Then if you decide you really do need your blenders, broilers, coffee makers, skillets, food mixers, toasters, electric toothbrushes, etc., this 11-page brochure will show you how to buy and care for them.

Send: a postcard
Ask for: "A Consumer's Guide to Portable Appliances"
Write to: Edison Electric Institute
1111 19th St., N.W.
Washington, D.C. 20036

Indoor Lighting

No matter how you decorate your home, lighting has the final say on mood, atmosphere, color scheme, and even heat and safety. "Lighting Ideas for Successful Decorating" helps you determine light needs for bathroom, kitchen, dining/living room and even outdoors. Diagrams show how to place lighting for aid in reading, working, playing pool, and even sophisticated dining.

Send: $1.00
Ask for: "Lighting Ideas for Successful Decorating"
Write to: Thomas Industries, Inc.
207 E. Broadway
Louisville, Ky. 40202

Antique Lamps

Antique lamps really complete the "country look" so many Americans want to achieve in their homes. A fold-out, "American Period Lighting Fixtures," contains drawings and photographs of 23 lanterns, postlights, chandeliers, and hall lights, made in such "old-fashioned" materials as brass, copper, tin, and pewter.

Send: $1.00
Ask for: "American Period Lighting Fixtures"
Write to: The Saltbox
2229 Marietta Pike
Lancaster, Pa. 17603

Chandeliers

If you're attracted to lighting, the King Chandelier Company will hold you spellbound with its fine collection of several hundred chandeliers and sconces. You'll see beautiful crystal pieces imported from Europe and read about such chandelier clients as Beverly Sills and Marina Svetlana.

Send: $1.00
Ask for: King's Chandelier Company Catalog
Write to: King Chandelier Company
Hwy. 14
Eden (Leaksville), N.C. 27288

Fans

For decorating ideas using ceiling fans, send for "Hunter Olde Tyme Ceiling Fans," a cata-

log featuring 35 fans for kitchens, dens, bathrooms, etc. "Hunter Ventilating and Circulating Fans" is a tastefully designed catalog with beautiful black-and-white photographs of all types of fans.

Send: $1.00, first title; a postcard, second title

Ask for: "Hunter Olde Tyme Ceiling Fans" or "Hunter Ventilating and Circulating Fans"

Write to: Robbins and Meyers, Inc.
Comfort Conditioning Division
2500 Frisco Ave.
Memphis, Tenn. 38114

Hunter olde tyme ceiling fans

Hunter ceiling fans are year-round energy savers that not only keep you cooler in summer but warmer in winter, too. For cold-weather use, operate the fan at slow speed to push rising warm air back down to the living/working area. This helps prevent heat stratification (a difference in temperatures between ceiling and floor) especially if your ceilings are high or vaulted.

Drapes

Installing and designing your own drapes can be an art—or a disaster. Do it right with "The OB/MASCO Guide to Beautiful Windows." This fully illustrated fold-out helps you choose a style of window treatment, measure windows, determine length of rod, and decide length and width of drapes.

Send: 25¢

Ask for: "The OB/MASCO Guide to Beautiful Windows"

Write to: OB/MASCO
2930 Maria St.
Compton, Calif. 90221

Blinds and Shades

Don't be blind to an infinite number of window treatment possibilities. "Window Magic" is a 27-page booklet with decorating ideas for windows in every room of the house. Learn how to measure windows for blinds, as well as how blinds help conserve energy.

Send: $1.00

Ask for: "Window Magic"

Window magic

High ceilings are a luxury that's harder and harder to find these days. Forget them if you live in a contemporary home or apartment building.

To make a low ceiling appear higher, hang your window treatment from the very top of the wall where it meets the ceiling. Don't use a constructed valance. Emphasize the vertical line by going all the way to the floor. Select fabrics with a vertical pattern if it fits with your scheme.

Colonial Locks

Spruce up your door with a colonial-style lock. "18th Century Colonial Lock Masters" is an attractive brochure that will give you ideas about the many styles and shapes of locks, knobs, and trim. Install a touch of early America in your home with an authentic reproduction that incorporates modern security functions.

Send: 50¢
Ask for: "18th Century Colonial Lock Masters"
Write to: Baldwin Hardware
Manufacturing Corp.
841 Wyomissing Blvd.
Box 82
Reading, Penn. 19603

Household Cutlery

Are some knives better for cold meats and some for hot meats? The answer to this and other interesting questions about cutlery are covered in "How to Choose and Care for Household Cutlery." Selecting the right style of knife for the right use and practical tips for sharpening and caring for knives are easily explained and illustrated in this handy fold-out.

Send: 25¢
Ask for: "How to Choose and Care
for Household Cutlery"
Write to: W.R. Case and Sons Cutlery Co.
20 Russell Blvd.
Bradford, Penn. 16701

Antiques

Browse through an antique store by sending for the "Sturbridge Yankee Workshop" catalog from Brimfield, Mass., the capital of flea markets. You'll find a myriad of old Americana, including brass wall clocks, porcelain dolls, stained glass, braided rugs, crocheted bedspreads, Colonial weathervanes, oak towel racks, and much, much more.

Send: a postcard
Ask for: "Sturbridge Yankee Workshop:
Essentially Americana"
Write to: Sturbridge Yankee Workshop
Brimfield Tpke.
Sturbridge, Mass. 01566

Specific Rooms and Areas

Rec Rooms

A family room is for fun—it's the perfect place for reading, relaxing, watching TV, playing games, or other family activities. If you have unused basement or attic space, you can design the perfect rec room. "Family and Rec Rooms," a 50-page booklet from *Better Homes and Gardens,* helps with all kinds of ideas for designing dens, music rooms, studies, etc.

Send: $1.25
Ask for: "Family and Rec Rooms"
Write to: National Plan Service
435 W. Fullerton Ave.
Elmhurst, Ill. 60126

Family and rec rooms

By the strictest definition, a family room is just for relaxing, reading, playing games, and watching television with the family. This means that every member should be considered; there should be a spot for Mom and Dad to read in quiet, a place for the kids to study, and room to watch favorite television shows.

Basement Rec Rooms

Right under your feet is some of the most wasted space in the household—the basement.

"Ideas for a Living Basement" shows you how to turn precious unused space into recreational areas the whole family can enjoy. These 19 pages of color ideas include room layouts and floor plans for workshops, model rooms, sewing centers, activities rooms, etc.

Send: 25¢
Ask for: "Ideas for a Living Basement"
Write to: The Bilco Co.
West Haven, Conn. 06505

Kitchen Cabinets

The "Do It Yourself Kitchen Guide" provides step-by-step instructions to help you plan the kitchen arrangement that best suits your family. This 12-page brochure, prepared by a

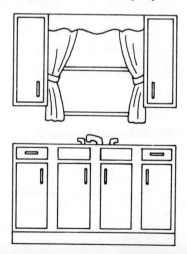

leading manufacturer of kitchen cabinets, focuses on the prominent place handsome and sturdy cabinets have in any kitchen redesigning project. Extra: kitchen cabinet plan-graph.

Send: $1.00
Ask for: "Do It Yourself Kitchen Guide"
Write to: 625 West Utica St.
Sellersburg, Ind. 47172

Kitchen Work Centers

No matter what our decorating preferences, a kitchen must always be functional first. "Functional Kitchens" is a 23-page booklet designed to help you plan efficient work centers in the kitchen. It determines points of heaviest kitchen traffic, organizes storage of food, and routes cooking and clean-up patterns.

Send: $1.50
Ask for: "Functional Kitchens" (NE-241)
Write to: Distribution Center, Dept. FHO
7 Research Park
Cornell University
Ithaca, N.Y. 14850

Kitchens

A well-planned kitchen is crucial for today's fast-paced lifestyle and two-career family. "Kitchen Planning," a 51-page booklet from *Better Homes and Gardens,* also brings such factors as lighting, ventilation, type of building materials, and even hobbies into play. Explore kitchen space planning and storage ideas for total decorating inspiration.

Send: $1.25
Ask for: "Kitchen Planning"

Write to: National Plan Service Inc.
435 W. Fullerton Ave.
Elmhurst, Ill. 60126

Kitchen planning

First, make a list of things you don't like about your present kitchen. Ask questions like these: Do too-low counters strain your back? Do you walk too much to prepare meals? Do you need new appliances, more storage space, or more room for eating?

Kitchens

If you don't feel your best in the kitchen, you need some KP—that is, kitchen planning. "Planning Tomorrow's Kitchen Today," a 12-page booklet from Whirlpool, helps you reshape your kitchen to make it a more efficient and pleasurable place to cook and entertain. Besides a section on before and after kitchen floor plans, there's a metric-conversion table and appliance-energy-savings tips.

Send: a postcard
Ask for: "Planning Tomorrow's Kitchen Today"

Write to: Whirlpool Corporation
Benton Harbor, Mich. 49022

Planning tomorrow's kitchen today

The kitchen is a creative, exciting, living place. Chances are, if you don't feel that way about your kitchen, you're not at your best there. Then it's time for some positive KP —Kitchen Planning.

Bathrooms

The bathroom is probably the most frequently used room in the house, and therefore needs to be maintained and updated often. "Bathroom Planning" helps you remodel your present bathroom, or add a half-bath to relieve family congestion. The 51 pages also include floor plans, photographs, and storage ideas.

Send: $1.25
Ask for: "Bathroom Planning"
Write to: National Plan Service
435 E. Fullerton Ave.
Elmhurst, Ill. 60126

Bathroom planning

Upstairs, downstairs, even in the basement you can find room for this unusually shaped bath. Because of its shape, it can fit neatly into several floor plan situations. The dimensions here are minimum; use more space if you can, but don't try anything smaller.

Kitchens and Bathrooms

For a kitchen planning guide with emphasis on storage, send for "Kitchen and Bath Planning—a Guide to Cabinet Selection" by Hildegarde Popper. Fifteen pages are devoted to kitchen design and plain talk about cabinets.

Send: 35¢
Ask for: "Kitchen and Bath Planning"
Write to: National Kitchen Cabinet
Association
136 St. Matthews Ave.
Louisville, Ky. 40207

Bathroom Design

The Poggenpohl-Bath 2000 catalog lends a European flair to bathroom design. Full-color photographs make these bathrooms look good enough to move right into. In 24 pages of floor plans and photos there are lots of visual decorating ideas.

Send: $1.00
Ask for: "The Poggenpohl-Bath 2000"
Write to: Poggenpohl
222 Cedar La.
Teaneck, N.J. 07666

Storage Problems

"Where do I put it all?" is the most common cry of the American homeowner. In answer to this question, *Better Homes and Gardens* has prepared a booklet, "Bookshelves and Storage," with unique and practical solutions to storage problems. Fifty-two pages help you locate, design, and build storage areas.

Send: $1.25
Ask for: "Bookshelves and Storage"

Write to: National Plan Service Inc.
435 W. Fullerton Ave.
Elmhurst, Ill. 60126

Bookshelves and storage

Most families' storage needs change constantly. At any given time, those needs are determined by the particular family's current interest, activities, and income, combined with the ages of the family members and number of people living in the home. Well-planned storage anticipates future needs while satisfying existing ones, thus adding to both the present and future value of the home.

Building Cedar Closets

Cedar closets don't just smell wonderful; they also repel moths, resist mildew, and store your clothes safely! For easy instructions on making your own, send for a fold-out, "Build Your Own Aromatic Cedar Closets," 4 closet pattern guides.
Send: 25¢
Ask for: "Build Your Own Aromatic
Cedar Closets

Write to: Giles and Kendall
P.O. Box 188
Huntsville, Ala. 35804

Storage

The makers of a shelving product have compiled a color booklet with hundreds of ideas for storing food, clothing, toys, books, plants, kitchen utensils, etc. This 16-page booklet, "Join Our Space Program," gives your extra items a lot of hang-ups.
Send: $1.00
Ask for: "Join Our Space Program"
Write to: Closet Maid Corporation
720 S.W. 17th St.
Ocala, Fla. 32670

Food Storage

Keeping a basic supply of food in your home is convenient and comforting, especially during unpredictable winter months, whether you grow your own produce or buy large-scale, vegetables and fruits picked and stored at peak-harvest time provide delicious, inexpensive, and nutritious meals for months to come. The lost art of natural winter refrigeration is revived in a 30-page booklet, "Home Storage of Fruits and Vegetables."
Send: $1.25
Ask for: "Home Storage of Fruits and
Vegetables" (NRAE-7)
Write to: Distribution Center, Dept. FHO
7 Research Park
Cornell University
Ithaca, N.Y. 14850

Exterior and Structural Maintenance

Exterior Repairs

A nail in time saves nine. It could also save you expensive labor costs. When repair problems are spotted right away, you can be your own handyman. "Simple home repairs ... Outside" assists you with precise step-by-step instructions and diagrams for fixing such common home problems as leaking roofs, loose shingles, unsealed joints, torn screens, broken window panes, clogged gutters, and more. Forty pages.

Send: $1.50
Ask for: "Simple Home Repairs ....Outside" (#1193)
Write to: Consumer Information Center Department Z Pueblo, Colo. 81009

Cedar Roof

Cedar is handsome, rigid yet resilient, and derives great structural strength from the overlapping method of its application. Cedar roofing makes your home warmer in winter and cooler in summer, lowering both your heating and air-conditioning bills. A 4-page brochure, "Put a New Cedar Roof Right Over Your Old Roof," teaches you how to roof with cedar.

Send: 10¢
Ask for: "Put a New Cedar Roof Right Over Your Old Roof"
Write to: Red Cedar Shingle & Handsplit Shake Bureau Suite 275 515 116th Ave. N.E. Bellevue, Wash. 98004

Roofing and Siding

For roofing and siding ideas, send for "What You Should Know About Roofing and Siding Before You Build or Remodel," 35 pages of homes using asphalt roofing and vinyl siding. Durability principles of these materials are emphasized.

Send: 50¢

Ask for: "What You Should Know About Roofing and Siding Before You Build or Remodel"

Write to: Bird & Son, Inc.
E. Walpole, Mass. 02032

Remodeling with Cedar

If you are thinking of remodeling your home with red cedar shingles or handsplit shakes, this new color brochure is packed with ideas. Photographs show remarkable step-by-step transformation of homes. Included are ideas from simple over-roofing to major remodeling.

Send: 25¢

Ask for: "Remodeling Ideas"

Write to: Red Cedar Shingle and Handsplit Shake Bureau
Suite 275
515 116th Ave., N.E.
Bellevue, Wash. 98004

Home Ventilation

If you have a stuffy room in your house, garage, shed or boat, you may need better ventilation. "Midget Louvers for Venting" will show how a simple little louvered vent can lower

heat and fume levels or provide a handy observation window.

Send: $1.00

Ask for: "Midget Louvers for Venting"

Write to: Midget Louver Co.
800 Main Ave., Route 7
Norwalk, Conn. 06852

Home upkeep and repair

Loose hinges (in doors) can usually be tightened by removing one screw at a time and replacing it with a longer screw. Or you can plug the hole with a toothpick or wooden matchstick and reinsert the original screw.

Waterproofing

A poster—"An Ounce of Prevention, a Pound of Cure"—works on the principle "a drop of water in time saves nine." Large drawings of a typical house and basement are marked with big black dots to indicate those spots you should waterproof immediately.

Send: 10¢

Ask for: "An Ounce of Prevention, a Pound of Cure"

Write to: Thoro System Products
Standard Dry Wall Products
7800 N.W. 38th St.
Miami, Fla. 33166

Fighting Corrosion

Four major types of corrosion faced by home-owners today are galvanic, crevice, pitting, and stress. "Corrosion—Facts for the Consumer," an 8-page booklet, first teaches you to recognize these destructive conditions and then tells how to slow, stop, and prevent corrosion on cast iron, aluminum, stainless steel, brass, bronze, silver, and more.

Send: $1.25
Ask for: "Corrosion—Facts for the
Consumer"
Write to: Consumer Information Center
Department Z
Pueblo, Colo. 81009

Corrosion facts for the consumer

The tarnish most often found on aluminum occurs in pots used to cook eggs or to heat certain types of tap water. This tarnish, usually a black or dark brown color, can be removed easily by cooking sour foods such as tart apples, sauerkraut, or tomatoes in the pot.

Wood-Decay

The Forest Service has put out a 24-page booklet about the nature of wood decay. "Your Wood Can Last for Centuries" shows you how and where decay begins in your house, and what to do about it.

Send: $1.00
Ask for: "Your Wood Can Last for
Centuries"
Write to: Superintendent of Documents
U.S. Government Printing Office
Washington, D.C. 20402

Your wood can last for centuries

Some houses built of wood endure for centuries; yet others develop decay problems soon after construction. Why? Because wood is a biological material. Used properly, it doesn't deteriorate. Misused, it succumbs to the same biological processes that decompose dead trees in the forest.

Fireplaces

After a brief fling with central heating and the TV set, Americans are returning to the hearth as a center of warmth and family fellowship. A fireplace not only saves money in heating

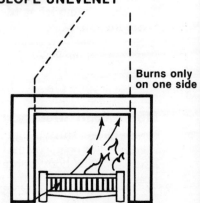

SIDES OF SMOKE CHAMBER SLOPE UNEVENLY

Burns only on one side

costs, it unifies the household and beautifies the home. "Common Fireplace Furnishings" will help you size up your living room, choose the right style of hearth; teach you how to build a fire, select the proper wood; and show you how to maintain your fireplace. A wall detail planning sheet, information on screens and accessories, and a brief history of fireplaces are included in 36 pages.

Send: $1.00
Ask for: "Common Fireplace Furnishings"
Write to: Portland Willamette Co.
6666 N.E. 59th Pl.
Portland, Ore. 97213

Fireplaces

If the sides of the smoke chamber are slanted at different angles, it will cause the fire to burn unevenly.

DAMPER SHORTER THAN FIREPLACE OPENING

Fireplaces

Nothing makes a home more comfortable and friendly than a fireplace. A blazing fire does more than almost anything else to make your home a cozy oasis of peace and quiet. A 52-page booklet, "Fireplaces," from *Better Homes and Gardens* magazine, tells you everything you always wanted to know about fireplaces, including information on the installation, maintenance, and use of nearly every type of fireplace. A handy book whether you already have a fireplace or are thinking of adding one.

Send: $1.25
Ask for: "Fireplaces"
Write to: National Plan Service Inc.
435 W. Fullerton Ave.
Elmhurst, Ill. 60126

Fireplaces

"Fireplaces and Chimneys" is a 23-page booklet designed to illustrate the proper construction of chimneys and fireplaces essential for safe, efficient operation. Not a do-it-yourself manual, it is aimed at providing the average homeowner with a working knowledge of fireplace construction so that he or she can follow the work of professionals in an informed manner and properly inspect and maintain the completed unit.

Send: $1.25
Ask for: "Fireplaces and Chimneys," (Farmer's Bulletin 1889)
Write to: Superintendent of Documents
U.S. Government Printing Office
Washington, D.C. 20402

Outdoor Places and Accessories

Landscaping

Owning several acres of land around your home means more land to enjoy—but more ground to develop. "Landscaping Around Home—Get Help, Plan Carefully" helps you consider such factors as direction of sun and wind, shape of plot, and natural or man-made features when analyzing your site for landscaping; 11 pages include helpful diagrams.

Send: a postcard
Ask for: "Landscaping Around Home—Get Help, Plan Carefully "(YS-78-5)
Write to: Superintendent of Documents
U.S. Government Printing Office
Washington, D.C. 20402

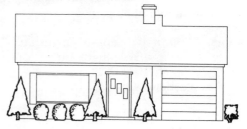

Landscaping around home—get help, plan carefully

The house exerts a strong influence on landscape design . . . Rarely are the house and garden designed together.
A door from the kitchen or dining room is the logical place for outdoor cooking and eating. A door from the living room to an outdoor patio is a logical place to sit or entertain. A door from a bedroom could lead to a private garden.

Landscaping

"Landscaping and Fencing" is a handy 51-page booklet covering all topics in landscaping. You literally start from scratch by learning how to diagram your lot, seed your lawn, plant new trees, shrubs, and flowers, and build fences and gates.
Send: $1.25

Ask for: "Landscaping and Fencing"
Write to: National Plan Service, Inc.
435 West Fullerton Ave.
Elmhurst, Ill. 60126

Write to: California Redwood Association
One Lombard St.
San Francisco, Calif. 94111

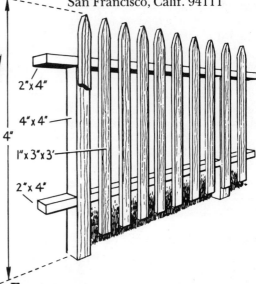

Landscaping and fencing

Before you plant a hedge, take time to consider the desired size, the maintenance required, and what the hedge should accomplish. Use informal hedges for screens; they require little care. Use formal hedges for property dividers or borders; they need regular shearing.

Redwood Fencing

"Building a Redwood Fence," a 6-page fold-out data sheet, will help you plan, construct and enjoy a redwood fence. It covers everything from local building codes, legal requirements for fencing a swimming pool, the problems of building a fence on a hilly or windy site and how to deal with neighbors when assigning costs to nails and finishes. There won't be much you don't know about building a redwood fence if you read this brochure thoroughly.

Send: 50¢
Ask for: "Building a Redwood Fence"

Fences

If you're still undecided about whether to put a fence around your property, a pamphlet, "On the Fence About Fencing," may be of help. This fold-out describes the durability, easy installation and low maintenance qualities of chain link fencing material.

Send: #10 self-addressed, stamped envelope
Ask for: "On the Fence About Fencing?"
Write to: Chain Link Fence Manufacturers Institute
Promotion Division (JW)
111 E. Wacker Dr.
Chicago, Ill. 60601

Trees and Shrubs

If you're contemplating adding trees or shrubbery to your property, "Cornell Home Garden Guide for Trees and Shrubs" will advise on planting, fertilizing, mulching, pruning, and watering for both deciduous and evergreen plants. This fold-out includes instructions for planting trees bare root, in ball and burlap, or in pot, pack, or container.

Send: 50¢
Ask for: "Cornell Home Garden Guide for Trees and Shrubs" (S-112)
Write to: Distribution Center
7 Research Park
Cornell University
Ithaca, N.Y. 14850

Pool fun

For a pool handbook with emphasis on *fun*, send for "Pool Ways." This 23-page booklet is full of pool-party ideas such as "wacky-water races" and beauty pageants for the whole neighborhood. "Easy Pool Recipes" let Mom and Dad in on the swim, while a "Pool Know-How Checklist" reminds you of simple pool maintenance.

Send: 50¢
Ask for: "Pool Ways"
Write to: Coastal Industries, Inc.
P.O. Box 363
Carlstadt, N.J. 07072

Landscaping Designs

The smaller your parcel, the more enjoyment per square foot your family will want from your land. "Landscape Design for Residential Property," 7 pages of plotting, helps you make the most of very little.

Send: 15¢
Ask for: "Landscape Design for Residential Property" (E-1099)
Write to: Distribution Center, Dept. FHO
7 Research Park
Cornell University
Ithaca, N.Y. 14850

Drainage Problems

Poor drainage around the home results in flooded basements, rotting foundations, swampy grounds, and drowned trees and plants. "Drainage Around the Home" is a 15-page booklet showing you how to correct

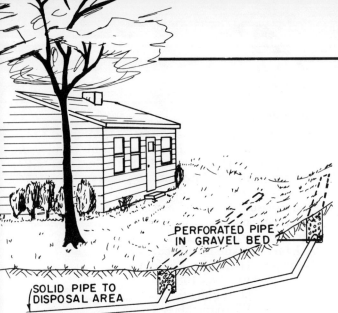

PERFORATED PIPE
IN GRAVEL BED

SOLID PIPE TO
DISPOSAL AREA

drainage problems around existing homes, and to evaluate drainage needs for homes under construction.

Send: 60¢
Ask for: "Drainage Around the Home" (IB-14)
Write to: Distribution Center, Dept. FHO
7 Research Park
Cornell University
Ithaca, N.Y. 14850

Awnings

Another energy-saver making a great comeback is the awning. Awnings block the sun's heat in summer, the wind's chill in winter. A 12-page booklet, "Sunbrella Fabrics Can Save Energy and Look Beautiful," offers some colorful awning design ideas for your windows.

Send: 50¢

Ask for: "Sunbrella Fabrics Can Save Energy and Look Beautiful"
Write to: Glen Raven Mills Inc.
Glen Raven, N.C. 27215

Sunbrella fabrics can save energy and look beautiful

The fact is, awnings block out more than 75% of the sun's heat, reducing room temperatures by 8 to 15 degrees. So air conditioners are used less often and at lower speeds. As a result, people can save up to an astonishing 25% on air conditioning costs.

Light Outdoor Structures

Why let construction costs put you in the doghouse when you can build your own? Hammond Barns "Build-It Plans for Fun or Profit" is a catalog of plans you can send away for. Includes light construction items such as barns, garages, bird feeders, doghouses, etc.

Send: a postcard
Ask for: "Build-It Plans for Fun or Profit"
Write to: Hammond Barns
Box 584
New Castle, Ind. 47362

Built It plans for fun or profit

Wheel barrow planter

Add beauty to your yard, patio or flower garden with this lovely wheel barrow planter. Very simple to build and can even be built from scrap material.

Weather Vanes

What do eagles, country doctors, sailboats, cows, whales, fire engines, golfers, French poodles, locomotives, Mallard ducks, automobiles and hansom cabs have in common? They're all on weather vanes. Learn how to select and mount your own in "Handcrafted Aluminum Weather Vanes." They're not just roosters anymore!

Send: $1.00
Ask for: "Handcrafted Aluminum Weather Vanes"
Write to: Wilson's Country House
Box 244
West Simsbury, Conn. 06092

Bird Feeders

Backyard bird-watchers will love "Hyde Bird Feeders—for Yards of Happiness." This catalog features imaginative and fun feeders that are strictly for the birds. Its 15 pages include advice on what to do about "bully birds" and "enterprising squirrels," as well as a bird food-preference chart.

Send: a postcard
Ask for: "Hyde Bird Feeders"
Write to: Hyde Bird Feeder Co.
P.O. Box 168
56 Felton St.
Waltham, Mass. 12254

Hyde bird feeders

The next time you are watching birds at your feeder, notice how they use their bills to feed. Each species in the great family of birds has a different kind of bill for its own special needs. There are long, sharp bills and broad, flat bills; rapier bills and shovel bills; hooked bills and straight bills.

Outdoor Wood Projects

Wood is beautiful, strong, versatile and a perfect building material for "All Weather Wood Outdoor Projects." This 16-page booklet from the Osmose Wood Preserving Co. of America offers colorful illustrated plans for patios, garden benches, fences, greenhouses and more.

Send: 50¢
Ask for: "All Weather Wood Outdoor Projects"

Write to: Osmose Wood Preserving Co. of
America, Inc.
980 Ellicott St.
Buffalo, N.Y. 14209

Outdoor Spaces

"Patios and Decks," a 52-page booklet from
Better Homes and Gardens, lets homeowners design their outdoor living spaces with as much
care as they would their indoors. After you
decide whether a patio or a deck would best
suit your needs, let a wealth of design possibilities inspire you, then follow practical construction details.
Send: $1.25
Ask for: "Patios and Decks"
Write to: National Plan Service
435 Fullerton Ave.
Elmhurst, Ill. 60126

Yard Projects with Wood

Now you can build that special outdoor project even easier than ever. "Outdoor Projects"
will give you 5 basic plans for a playhouse, play
center, chaise lounge, storage area, and
planter. These plans plus your own touches
and preferences will go a long way to making
your project run smoothly.
Send: a postcard
Ask for: "Outdoor Projects"
Write to: Georgia-Pacific
900 S.W. Fifth Ave.
Portland, Ore. 97204

Yard Decks

Here are 5 easy-to-build decks from Georgia-
Pacific, including plans, materials lists and
helpful hints. Touch up a corner of your yard
with sturdy wood decks that look elaborate but
are easy to construct and that will make your
yard the hit of the neighborhood.
Send: a postcard
Ask for: "Decks"
Write to: Georgia-Pacific
900 S.W. Fifth Ave.
Portland, Ore. 97204

Redwood Decks

A brochure from California Redwood Association, "Redwood Decks—Do It!," will give you
many colorful ideas for your own deck design.
Once built, "Redwood Deck Finishes" will in-
struct you on waterproofing, staining, or
bleaching your new deck for years of long-
lasting wear and use.

Send: 50¢ each
Ask for: "Redwood Decks—Do It!"
"Redwood Deck Finishes"
Write to: California Redwood Association
One Lombard St.
San Francisco, Calif. 94111

Garden Pools

Water adds a touch of mystery and fun to any garden. "Redwood Garden Settings for Spas, Tubs, Pools" shows in luxurious color photos what wood can do to make a garden into an oasis. Put a spa or pool in your garden and see the difference.
Send: 50¢
Ask for: "Redwood Garden Settings for Spas, Tubs, Pools"
Write to: California Redwood Association
One Lombard St.
San Francisco, Calif. 94111

Hot Tubs

"Hot Tubbing, The Scene and the People," a good-looking booklet from California Cooperage, tells you just about everything you could ever want to know about hot tubs. From installation (including something for the do-it-yourselfer) to maintenance and accessories—it's all here. If you've been wondering if the hot tub experience is for you, you can find out with the help of this brochure. It's fun, factual, and fantastic!
Send: $1.00
Ask for: "Hot Tubbing, The Scene and the People"

Write to: California Cooperage
800 Industrial Way
Box E
San Luis Obispo, Calif. 93406

Pool Care

Pools are fun, but need care to keep them clean and safe. E-Z "Pool Care Guide" shows you how to determine pool capacity, PH content, alkalinity, algae content and common pool problems. These 18 useful pages pool such topics as water testing, chlorination and stabilization, pool opening and closing, and vocabulary.
Send: a postcard
Ask for: "E-Z Clor Pool Care Guide"
Write to: E-Z Clor Pool Care Products
A Division of Airwick Pool Products
4 Cermak Blvd.
St. Peters, Mo. 63376

Underground Sprinklers

You don't have to rely on Mother Nature or drag a heavy hose around when your lawn needs a drink. Learn the advantages of underground sprinkler systems—and how to install one that meets your yard's needs—in "How to

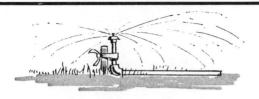

Plan, Layout, and Install Rain Jet Underground Sprinklers." It's just like rain.

Send: 25¢

Ask for: "How to Plan, Layout, and Install Rain Jet Underground Sprinklers"

Write to: Rain Jet Corp.
301 S. Flower St.
Burbank, Calif. 91503

Well Water

Well water is plentiful, fresher, and more economical than public systems. A pamphlet, "Understanding Underground Water," explains wells, pumps, and complete home water systems, as well as how to size a pump.

Send: 45¢

Ask for: "Understanding Underground Water"

Write to: Water Systems Council
221 North La Salle St.
Chicago, Ill. 60601

Wells/Water Systems

If you are thinking of having a well dug on your property and want to read up on the state of the art, "Order Your Water Well Done" is the booklet for you. Neither a technical man-

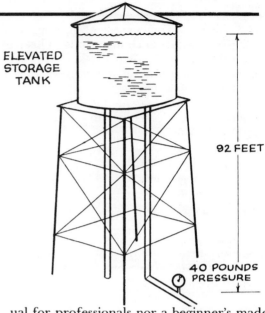

ELEVATED STORAGE TANK

92 FEET

40 POUNDS PRESSURE

ual for professionals nor a beginner's made-easy guide, this 28-page booklet covers the middle ground on such topics as locating, constructing and sizing the water system.

Send: 75¢

Ask for: "Order Your Water Well Done"

Write to: Water Systems Council
221 North La Salle St.
Chicago, Ill. 60601

Greenhouses

Solar heating does *not* have to mean motors, flat-plate collectors, heat-transfer devices, or parabolic mirrors. A simple glass structure can let sun in to heat cement walls of the house that will give off warmth all night long. This passive solar heating system is what an 8-page brochure, "It Runs on the Sun—and Not Much Else," is all about.

Send: a postcard
Ask for: "It Runs on the Sun—and Not Much Else"
Write to: Vegetable Factory, Inc.
100 Court St.
Copiague, N.Y. 11726

It runs on the sun

Foundations don't help plants grow, they're expensive insurance to protect glass from breaking when ground freezes and "heaves" in winter . . . With a greenhouse of completely shatterproof walls, a simple, inexpensive set of stakes or anchor bolts is all that is required.

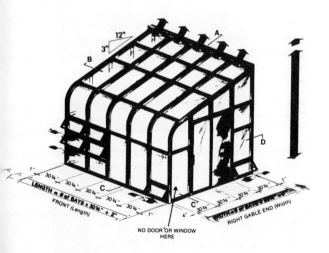

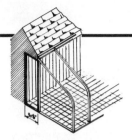

(SIDE FILLER KIT)

Greenhouses

To find out about a home addition that heats the house, grows plants, and provides a sun-basking area all year round, write for the "Four Seasons Passive Solar Greenhouse and Add-a-Room" brochure. Fourteen pages include photographs, information, solar-energy heating charts, and an offer for free description plans of the Brookhaven House.

Send: $1.00
Ask for: "The Four Seasons Passive Solar Greenhouse and Add-a-Room"
Write to: Four Seasons Solar Products Corp.
910 Route 110
Farmingdale, N.Y. 11735

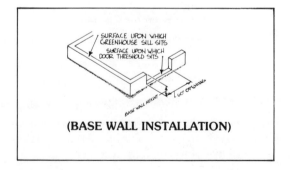

(BASE WALL INSTALLATION)

Tools, Paints, and Other Materials

Tools

For a complete "Gray's Anatomy" of tools, send for the "Stanley Tool Guide." This extremely useful handbook dissects dozens of tools, while identifying and determining usage of their different parts and accessories. The 39 pages also teach you how to use measuring and marking tools, try squares and marking gauges, and identify common cuts of wood and wood joints.

Send: 75¢
Ask for: "Stanley Tool Guide" (94-615)
Write to: Stanley Tools
The Stanley Works
New Britain, Conn. 06050

Stanley tool guide

Use the longest screw driver convenient for the work. More power can be applied to a long screw driver than a short one, with less danger of its slipping out of the slot.

If no hole is bored for the threaded part of the screw the wood is often split or the screw is twisted off. If a screw turns too hard, back it out and enlarge the hole. A little soap on the threads of the screw makes it easier to drive.

Troweling

There is one tool for people of all walks of life —the trowel. A booklet called "Troweling Tips and Techniques" teaches you how to get the most out of this handy tool in all sidewalk, concrete wall, and bricklaying jobs in 24 pages of step-by-step instructions with accompanying diagrams.

Send: 75¢
Ask for: "Troweling Tips and Techniques"

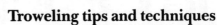

Write to: Marshalltown Trowel Co.
P.O. Box 738
Marshalltown, Iowa 50158

Troweling tips and techniques

Brick should be moist but not wet. Too much moisture will dilute the mortar and cause bricks to slip in the mortar bed. To assure proper moisture spray bricks late in the day preceding use . . . and early in the morning (about 4 hours before) if you intend to lay them later the same day.

Masonry

Imaginative masonry and concrete work can be used in myriad ways to build distinctive houses and enhance exteriors. The building of patios, decorative walls, pools, brick walks, fireplaces, and driveways—from the first plan to the finished work—is clearly explained, step by step. "Masonry and Concrete," a 50-page booklet, is a valuable aid to the do-it-yourselfer.

Send: $1.25
Ask for: "Masonry and Concrete"
Write to: National Plan Service
435 Fullerton Ave.
Elmhurst, Ill. 60126

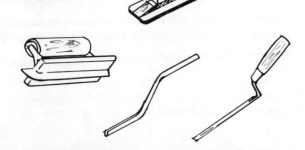

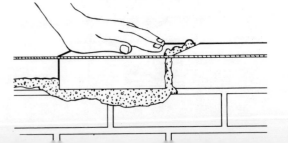

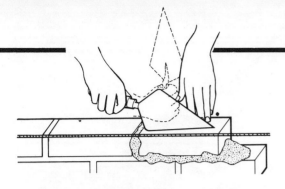

Masonry and concrete

Driveways should be 3 feet wider than any vehicle that will use them . . . On a sloping lot, make the curve of the drive gradual, building up the driveway base or digging it deeper as necessary, so a car will not drag on a bump or strike its bumper on a too-abrupt curve.

Tool Rental

When you need special tools for big jobs around the house, don't beg, borrow, or steal —or botch up the job! "Need It—Rent It!" is a booklet put out by the American Rental Association to help you get professional results *and* keep your friends. Advice on operating machines includes such large tools as floor sanders, power leaf vacuums, hedge trimmers, shampoo machines, engine hoists, chain saws, and more.

Send: a postcard
Ask for: "Need It—Rent It!"
Write to: American Rental Association
1900 19th St.
Moline, Ill. 61265

Need it, rent it

When working on hilly ground:

Always stand on uphill side of log when cutting. After completing a cut, wait for chain to stop before moving the saw.

Power Tools

If you've been saving money being your own handyman or -woman, an investment in power tools can also save you valuable time, as well as improve the quality of your work. "Power Hand Tools" removes confusion about what kind of tools to buy, teaches you how to use them, and acquaints you with parts and accessories in 24 pages. Drawings and diagrams of drills, sanders, and saws undo the "puzzle" of power tools to let you use them safely and efficiently.

Send: 40¢
Ask for: "Power Hand Tools"
Write to: Consumer Information
Public Documents Distribution
Center
Pueblo, Colo. 81009

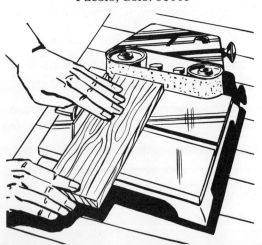

Lawn Mowers

Homeowners tend to forget how dangerous the power lawn mower can be. "Lawn Power Equipment" teaches you in 16 pages how to use this tool safely and effectively. Extra 4-H Club bonuses: quiz sheets on operating, using, and storing equipment, as well as a record chart for expenses.

Send: 20¢
Ask for: "Lawn Power Equipment" (M-2-8a)
Write to: Distribution Center, Dept. FHO
7 Research Park
Cornell University
Ithaca, N.Y. 14850

Painting Tips

Painting not only keeps your home looking its best, it also protects it against damage. Doing the job yourself can save you money, but make sure you first read "Painting—Inside and Out." This 24-page booklet shows you how to choose the right paint, prepare surfaces for painting, and then apply it correctly and efficiently. Paint selection charts tell you what paint to choose for painting on brick, concrete, steel, wood, or vinyl.

Send: $1.30
Ask for: "Painting—Inside and Out" (#222)
Write to: Consumer Information Center
Department Z
Pueblo, Colo. 81009

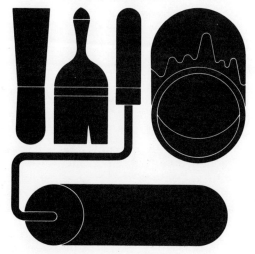

Painting inside and out

End each stroke with a light, lifting motion. Paint along the grain of wood. When you finish an area, go over it with light, quick strokes to smooth any minor marks and to recoat any unnoticed thin spots.

Primer Sealers

You're all set to paint and someone asks, "Did you use a primer sealer?" Don't panic. "When and Where to Use a Primer Sealer" will explain the differences between porous and non-porous surfaces, and how to treat problems and special surfaces. You'll also learn helpful hints for easier painting.

Send: a postcard
Ask for: "When and Where to Use a Primer Sealer"
Write to: William Zinsser and Co.
39 Bélmont
Somerset, N.J. 08873

When and where to use a primer sealer

Primer-sealers should be stirred thoroughly before use so that no settled pigment remains on the bottom of the can. Failure to disperse the pigment thoroughly will adversely affect both the sealing and the priming function.

Paint

Skimmed cow's milk and buttermilk have been used in paintmaking for several thousand years. Here's a company which produces a milk paint with the look of the old-fashioned variety, but with the staying power of modern technology. "The Old-Fashioned Milk Paint Catalog" features actual paint samples and an interesting look at an unusual and authentic operation.

Send: 60¢

Ask for: "The Old-Fashioned Milk Paint Catalog"

Write to: The Old-Fashioned Milk Paint Co.
Box 222
Groton, Mass. 01450

Old-fashioned milk paint catalog

Skimmed cow's milk and buttermilk have been used as a vehicle and binder in paints for several thousand years. The Egyptians were known to use skim milk, quicklime and earth colors to brighten their buildings. From the Middle Ages up to quite recently, itinerant house painters traveled throughout Europe with their coloring materials. The housewife would save skim milk and let it curdle before the painter arrived to mix and apply the paint.

Painting

If you'd rather start painting than reading about it, "Paint & Painting" will give you advice in as few words as possible. Turn right to your section (using a brush? using a roller? using a sprayer?), prepare your surface (wood? masonry? metal?), know where you are (inside? outside?), and go. Just be sure to check the "What to Use and Where" chart. Also included in the 23 pages is a color scheme chart, to match trim and main colors.

Send: 85¢

Ask for: "Paint & Painting"

Write to: Superintendent of Documents
U.S. Government Printing Office
Washington, D.C. 20402

Painting

"How to Paint," a pocket-sized packet of 7 folders from Pratt and Lambert, describes materials and techniques to help you achieve professional looking results on your next painting project. This mini library covers interior painting, exterior painting, floor finishing, wood finishing, antiquing, super-graphic painting, and even how to paint your swimming pool.

Send: $1.00

Ask for: "How to Paint" Mini Library

Write to: Pratt and Lambert
P.O. Box 22
Buffalo, NY. 14240

Cement

Before you pour it on, know what you're talking about! The "Sakrete Cement Mixes Instruction Booklet" helps you establish a permanent relationship with cement structures for posts, steps, patios, flower-bed edges, walls, pools, sidewalks, and more, with 15 pages of instructions and illustrations.

Send: 50¢

Ask for: "Sakrete Cement Mixes Instruction Booklet"

Write to: Sakrete, Inc.
P.O. Box 17087
Cincinnati, Ohio 45217

Energy Conservation

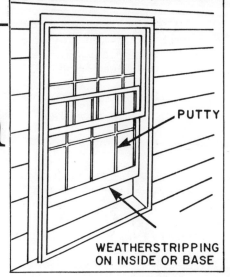

PUTTY

WEATHERSTRIPPING
ON INSIDE OR BASE

Energy Workbook

A think-and-do approach to energy-conservation is "Home Energy Saver's Workbook." Its 28 pages include energy quizzes, charts for computing fuel costs, cooling savings, draft factors, etc., plus, "How to Calculate Your First Floor Area and Heated Living Area."

Send: $1.00
Ask for: "Home Energy Saver's Workbook" (FEA/D-77/117)
Write to: Superintendent of Documents
U.S. Government Printing Office
Washington, D.C. 20402

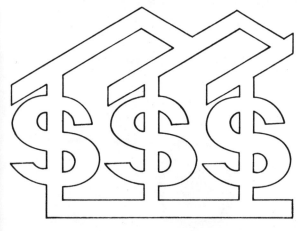

Home energy saver's workbook

Homeowners, like other consumers, are often victims of a lack of information. It is sometimes difficult to determine how serious a problem a malfunctioning furnace, termites, or faulty plumbing might be—and consequently, how much a homeowner should invest to correct such problems.

Energy Efficiency

Saving energy does not have to go hand-in-hand with physical discomfort. By making your home energy-efficient, you save money without losing warmth. For a booklet full of charts and information on budgeting heating costs, send for "Making the Most of Your Energy Dollars."

Send: 70¢
Ask for: "Making the Most of Your Energy Dollars"

Write to: Superintendent of Documents
U.S. Government Printing Office
Washington, D.C. 20402

Making the most of your energy dollars

Did you know? Most of the 40 million owner-occupied houses in the United States could use additional insulation to offset sharply rising energy prices. This is especially true of the majority of houses built before the 1960's and those with air conditioning units added after the house was completed.

Water Conservation

A 7-page pamphlet from the Department of Agriculture, "Water Conservation Checklist for the Home," helps you become a better manager of your water resources. The checklist includes an astonishing variety of water-saving suggestions. Learn tricks for food preparation, laundry, gardening, and personal care, all designed to preserve your standard of living but cut *way* back on your daily water consumption.

Send: 70¢
Ask for: "Water Conservation Checklist for the Home" (PA-1192)
Write to: Superintendent of Documents
U.S. Government Printing Office
Washington, D.C. 20402

Retrofit

"Retrofit" is a word we'll all be hearing more of in the future. It is used to cover all those renovations done to save energy, such as weatherstripping, insulation, and maintenance of mechanical and water heating systems. Learn about energy remodeling from a contractor's point of view in a 22-page booklet, "Ever Heard of Retrofit?"

Send: $1.10
Ask for: "Ever Heard of Retrofit?"
(DOE/CS-0001)
Write to: Superintendent of Documents
U.S. Government Printing Office
Washington, D.C. 20402

Ever hear of retrofit?

The word retrofit is used to cover all those renovations that are done to save energy . . . caulking and weather-stripping; storm windows and storm doors; attic insulation; wall insulation; underfloor insulation; maintenance of mechanical systems; maintenance of water heating systems.

Energy Conservation

With fossil fuels continuing to dwindle at a steady rate, energy-conscious Americans now need to be energy misers. "Save Energy, Save Dollars" teaches you to make your house as energy-efficient as possible without sacrificing personal comfort. Energy-conservation tips on everything from home insulation to hot water usage not only save you precious heating costs, but put you in control of energy consumption in your home. Helpful diagrams and an energy management checklist are included in this 95-page workbook!

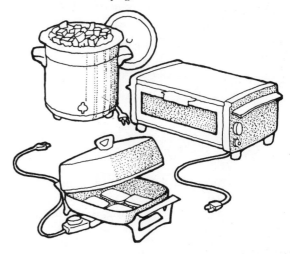

Send: $1.50
Ask for: "Save Energy, Save Dollars"
(IB-125)
Write to: Distribution Center, Dept. FHO
7 Research Park
Cornell University
Ithaca, N.Y. 14853

Energy Tips

A direct approach to saving energy in and around the home is "Tips for Energy Savers." No lecture, just the straight scoop on cutting down wasteful consumption in 29 pages that cover just about everything, including insulation, heating, air conditioning, utilities, appliances, lighting, car maintenance, travel, even advice on what to look for when shopping for, or building a house. A must for every home-owner.

Send: a postcard
Ask for: "Tips for Energy Savers"
(DOE/OPA-0037)
Write to: Consumer Information Center
Department Z
Pueblo, Colo. 81009

Skylights

Skylights save energy by reducing the need for artificial lighting and add enormously to the aesthetic pleasure of living and working indoors. Modern skylight fabrication techniques have reduced the cooling and heating loss which caused concern in the past. Learn how the use of skylights can improve your lifestyle —this small fold-out can help.

Send: 30¢ and a self-addressed stamped
envelope

Ask for: "Shedding Light on Energy Savings with Skylights"
Write to: Architectural Aluminum Manufacturers Assn.
35 E. Wacker Dr.
Chicago, Ill. 60601

Energy Conservation

Here is the "Big Ten Checklist"—proven ways for you to conserve energy and money. Individual efforts *do* count: the federal government says that if all Americans operated energy-efficient homes, the nation could save more than 1.5 million barrels of crude oil per day! In a brief fold-out, "Energy Conservation Begins At Home," check the value of weather-stripping, clock thermostats, insulation wraps for water heaters, storm doors and windows, and lots more.
Send: a postcard
Ask for: "Energy Conservation Begins At Home"
Write to: Committee for Home Energy Conservation
National Institute of Building Sciences
Suite 700, 1015 15th St., N.W.
Washington, D.C. 20005

Energy Saving

A little energy booklet with emphasis on savings in home heating is "Energy Savers." This 16-page pamphlet by the Burnham Corporation shows you where you may be wasting precious energy in home construction features and heating systems. An "Energy Waster Checklist" is included.
Send: a postcard
Ask for: "Energy Savers"
Write to: Burnham Corporation
Hydronics Division
Lancaster, Pa. 17604

Energy Checklist

Don't wait until it's too late—or too expensive—to install energy-saving features in homes when building or renovating. The "Energy-Saving Checklist for Home Builders, Buyers, and Owners" will help!
Send: a postcard
Ask for: "Energy-Saving Checklist for Home Builders, Buyers, and Owners" (DOE/OPA-0049)
Write to: DOE Technical Information Center
P.O. Box 62
Oak Ridge, Tenn. 37830

Energy Saving

Can you think of 94 ways to start saving energy in and around the home? Test your "energy I.Q." with a 6-page fold-out, "Energy Management Checklist for the Home." When you can check off all energy-saving suggestions, give yourself 100!
Send: 75¢
Ask for: "Energy Management Checklist for the Home" (PA-1118)
Write to: Superintendent of Documents
U.S. Government Printing Office
Washington, D.C. 20402

Heating and Insulation

Electric Heating

Electric energy waste is the topic in "Guide to Wise Use of Energy for Electric Heating and Cooling." Find out about heating systems that can be controlled—such as electric baseboards, radiant ceiling heat, floor insert heaters, wall and ceiling units, etc.—as well as other electricity-saving tips.

Send: a postcard
Ask for: "Guide to Wise Use of Energy for Electric Heating and Cooling"
Write to: Edison Electric Institute
1140 Connecticut Ave., N.W.
Washington, D.C. 20036

Home Heating

In an age when it is crucial to reduce energy use and costs, "Home Heating: Systems, Fuels, Controls" is the handbook that will show you how to do it. Learn the differences between warm-air and steam heating, the advantages and disadvantages of wood, coal, oil, gas, electricity; and all-important ways to reduce fuel consumption.

Send: $1.10
Ask for: "Home Heating: Systems, Fuels, Controls" (153H)
Write to: Consumer Information Center
Dept. Z
Pueblo, Colo. 81009

Water Heaters

A little fold-out wrapping up the subject of water heater insulation is "Insulate Your Water Heater and Save Fuel." Find out how to save money on utility bills with an insulation refit kit.

Send: a postcard
Ask for: "Insulate Your Water Heater and Save Fuel"
Write to: DOE—Technical Information Center
P.O. Box 62
Oak Ridge, Tenn. 37830

Humidification

Humidification during the winter months not only means greater comfort for you, it helps to protect the home and its furnishings from the harmful effects of dry air. Humidification reduces undesirable wintertime static electricity, as well as health problems resulting from dry nasal passages. The popularity of home

humidification has grown rapidly in recent years and this booklet is designed to help you decide whether or not you should select a humidifier as part of your home comfort package.

Send: a postcard
Ask for: "Humidification Facts"
Write to: Research Products Corp.
Madison, Wisc. 53701

Heating/Cooling Equipment

Wouldn't it be nice to have a system that heats, cools, humidifies, filters, and keeps a steady air flow through your home? A 16-page booklet, "How to Get the Most from Your Comfort Investment," describes this system.

Send: 50¢
Ask for: "How to Get the Most from Your Comfort Investment"
Write to: Lennox Industries, Inc.
P.O. Box 400450
Dallas, Tex. 75240

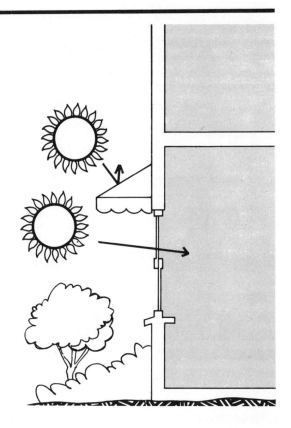

Insulation Tips

A booklet with emphasis on R-values of insulating materials is "Insulating Your Home" from the *Better Homes and Gardens* series. Learn about vapor barriers, ventilation, caulking, weatherstripping, and insulating attics, floors, crawl spaces, basements, and walls. Do-it-yourself instructions and diagrams.

Send: $1.25
Ask for: "Insulating Your Home"
Write to: National Plan Service
435 W. Fullerton Ave.
Elmhurst, Ill. 60126

Insulation

Adding styrofoam insulation to the outside of your home is an easy way to increase its insulation value. If you can handle a hammer and saw, "How to Insulate the Outside of Your Basement, Crawl Space, or Foundation Walls" will show you how to do it. You'll benefit from greater living comfort and lower heating and air-conditioning bills.
Send: a postcard

Ask for: "How to Insulate the Outside of Your Basement, Crawl Space, or Foundation Walls"
Write to: Dow Chemical U.S.A.
Styrofoam Brand Products
2020 Dow Center
Midland, Mich. 48640

Home Insulation

Chances are your home was built during the days when energy was cheap, and now you're losing precious heat through walls, ceilings, and floors. "How to Save Money by Insulating Your Home" remedies this problem with instructions on where and how you should insu-

late and weatherstrip, as well as what tools to use, and precautions to take.

Send: 40¢
Ask for: "How to Save Money by Insulating Your Home"
Write to: Mineral Insulation Manufacturers Assoc.
382 Springfield Ave.
Summit, N.J. 07901

How to save money by insulating your home

The amount of savings depends upon the climate you live in, the amount of insulation you install, the amount you had before you added more, the type and size of your house, your living habits, and family size. Your local utility company is a good source of information on what savings would be for you.

Home Insulation

Insulation has become a standard "energy" vocabulary term, but do you really understand what it is, and how it should be installed? "Questions and Answers on Home Insulation" clarifies any doubts you may have about the nature of the material, and how it should be used safely and efficiently.

Send: $1.10
Ask for: "Questions and Answers on Home Insulation"
Write to: Superintendent of Documents
U.S. Government Printing Office
Washington, D.C. 20402

Questions and answers on home insulation

When you talk to a contractor or are trying to decide for yourself how much insulation to buy, talk R-Values, not inches. R stands for Resistance to the flow of heat. The R-Value of any material is a measure of how good an insulator it is; that is, how well it resists the flow of heat into a home in summer or out of it in winter.

Solar Water Heating

Learn how a solar water heater works, how much it costs to build one (with different specifications given for a variety of climates), how much you'll actually save on utility bills, and how to choose the right system. A 7-page booklet, "Is Solar Water Heating Right for You?," is a good starting place as you set out to learn more about the possible benefits of solar power.

Send: a postcard
Ask for: "Is Solar Water Heating Right for You?" (HUD-PDR-577)
Write to: Superintendent of Documents
U.S. Government Printing Office
Washington, D.C. 20402

Is solar water heating right for you?

Why do you need two water heaters?

Whether one or two tanks are used, solar energy really serves to *preheat* the household hot water. At night and on cloudy days, the conventional backup heater gives the water a boost to the desired temperature.

Solar Energy

Sunlight as an energy source is the topic of a short brochure, "Solar Energy Facts." This 15-page booklet, put out by Research Products Corp., explores solar heating possibilities, offers a glossary of solar-energy terminology, and illustrates various solar-energy systems.

Send: a postcard
Ask for: "Solar Energy Facts"
Write to: Research Products Corp.
Box 1467
Madison, Wisc. 53701

Solar Heating

More information on passive solar heating with emphasis on process, rather than design, is in "Passive Solar Heating of Buildings" from Cornell University. This 4-page fold-out combines the warmth of the sun with insulation for successful solar heating ideas.

Send: 15¢
Ask for: "Passive Solar Heating of Buildings" (NRAE-FS-9)
Write to: Distribution Center, Dept. FHO
7 Research Park
Cornell University
Ithaca, N.Y. 14850

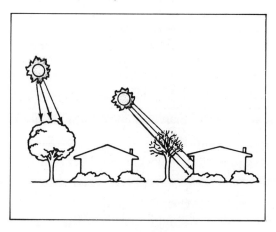

Solar energy and your home

There are four reasons why you should consider installing such a system in your home:
—You will have long-term savings.
—Your home may have a higher resale value as conventional energy prices increase.
—You will conserve energy.
—Your system will be ecologically safe and clean.

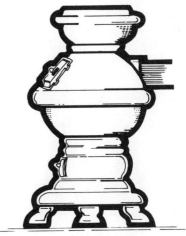

Antique Pot Belly

Solar Energy

Anyone investigating the use of solar energy for home heating should check "Solar Energy and Your Home." This 20-page booklet answers 29 questions on the benefits and uses of home solar heating systems. Included are a solar energy reading list, and references for additional information.

Send: a postcard
Ask for: "Solar Energy and Your Home"
Write to: National Solar Heating and
Cooling Information Center
P.O.Box 1607
Rockville, Md. 20850

Wood Burners

Wood is making a comeback across the nation as a source of fuel. Learn about types of wood, moisture content, operating a stove or fireplace, starting and maintaining a fire, chimney cleaning, etc., from an extremely informative

21-page booklet, "Heating With Wood." Diagrams, guidelines, and checklist.
Send: a postcard
Ask for: "Heating With Wood"
(#DOE/CS 0158)
Write to: DOE Technical Information
Center
P.O. Box 62
Oak Ridge, Tenn. 37830

Three Stages of Combustion

1. Moisture in wood driven off

2. Pyrolysis breaks wood into coals and gases

3. Coals and gases burn

Woodstoves

A pretty little booklet on wood stoves is the "Cawley/LeMay 400 and 600 Wood Stoves" catalog. Besides drawings and photographs of wood stoves, there's information on cooking and chimneys, installation, upkeep, and firing, plus firewood and safety. The 32 pages include diagrams and instructions on where to get additional information.
Send: $1.00
Ask for: "Cawley/LeMay 400 and
600 Wood Stoves"
Write to: The Cawley Stove Co.
27 N. Washington St.
Boyertown, Pa. 19512

Wood Fires

A booklet on wood fires with emphasis on family use and cooking is "The Warmth of Wood Fires" by James Titus. Twenty pages

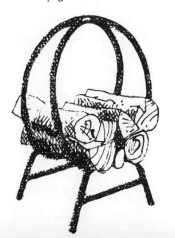

discuss such topics as dressing in homes with wood fires, children and safety, storage of wood, building a fire, and temperature control in cooking on your stove. An extra plus: recipes for stove-top cooking and baking.

Send: $1.25

Ask for: "The Warmth of Wood Fires" (IB-150)

Write to: Distribution Center, Dept. FHO
7 Research Park
Cornell University
Ithaca, N.Y. 14850

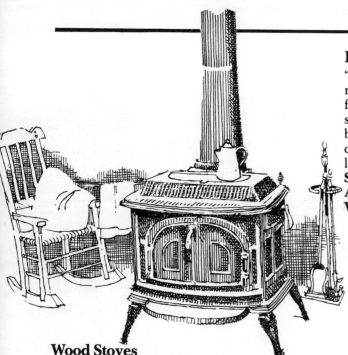

Heating with Wood

"Burning Wood" explains how to utilize this natural resource as a heating fuel in stoves, fireplaces, and furnaces. You'll learn how to season and store wood, install your own wood-burning apparatus, and even the correct procedures for felling a tree and chopping it into logs.

Send: $1.00
Ask for: "Burning Wood" (NE-191)
Write to: Distribution Center, Dept. FHO
7 Research Park
Cornell University
Ithaca, N.Y. 14850

Wood Stoves

Hot news: "Homeowners Turn to Stoves as Home Heating Costs Soar!" Also get the scoop on "more heat with less wood," "what features you should look for when shopping for a wood stove," "wood stove installation and safety," "general information concerning chimneys," etc. Order your copy of "The Woodburner" today.

Send: $1.00 if you write, free if you call 802-728-3111
Ask for: "The Woodburner"
Write to: All Nighter Stove Works
80 Commerce St.
Glastonbury, Conn. 06033

Wood and Coal

Why would you want a wood stove? Maybe you want to save money on your heating bills—a good wood stove will probably save you more than its purchase price within the first two heating seasons. A wood stove also represents security in a time when power outages are a matter of real concern. In this 24-page brochure, "Making Sense out of Wood Stoves and Coal Stoves," the Hayes Equipment Corp. describes the benefits you can realize from the installation of a wood stove.

Send: $1.00

Ask for: "Making Sense out of Wood Stoves and Coal Stoves"

Write to: Hayes Equipment Corp.
P.O. Box 526
150 New Britain Ave.
Unionville, Conn. 06085

Making sense out of wood stoves and coal stoves

In descending order of heat content, here are the best woods for your stove: apple, beech, elm, hickory, locust, white oak, white ash, birch, cherry, sugar maple, red oak and walnut.

Health and Safety

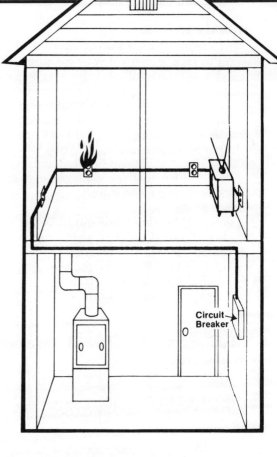

Circuit Breaker

Fire Safety

If your house was built between 1964 and 1973, you may have a serious fire hazard. A pamphlet entitled "Was Your Home Built After 1964?" calls your attention to clues to this potential hazard, caused by faulty aluminum wiring installed in many homes during this period.

Send: $1.25
Ask for: "Was Your Home Built After 1964?"
Write to: U.S. Consumer Product Safety Commission
Washington, D.C. 20207

Fire Safety

We read and hear about fires every day; yet our temptation is to believe, "It couldn't happen to me!" The danger here is that we then don't prepare ourselves. Education about fire is what "People and Fire" is all about. This 27-page booklet helps you plan for survival, with information on family evacuation, warning systems, escape routes, and fire fighting. Also: household materials most sensitive to fire, electrical troubleshooter's guide, and a household fire safety checklist.

Send: $1.40
Ask for: "People and Fire" (HUD-PDR-121-4)
Write to: U.S. Department of Housing and Urban Development
Washington, D.C. 20410

People and fire

Costume and party dresses worn at children's parties are especially dangerous around lighted candles and flames. Use candles sparingly and keep paper hats, dresses or long hair away from them. Don't leave candles burning unattended while you're away or asleep.

Aerosols

"Safe Use of Aerosols Around the House" is a short fold-out designed to help homeowners in the wise use and safe storage of some of the many useful household products which come in aerosol cans. A detailed description of just how an aerosol container works is accompanied by warnings about possible hazards if these containers are misused or mishandled.

Send: a postcard
Ask for: "Safe Use of Aerosols Around the House"
Write to: Aerosol Education Bureau
1001 Connecticut Ave., N.W.
Washington, D.C. 20036

Winter Emergencies

In "Winter Survival," emergency information is provided on what to do if the power goes out, how to deal with exposure, what if a blizzard traps you inside an automobile. Twenty pages also show you how to winterize your home for maximum comfort, safety, and economy, and offer good tips for clothing, bedding and even snack foods. A safe and

Home Air Pollution

Pollution is everywhere—even in the air we normally consider *fresh* outdoor air. The solutions to outdoor air pollution are difficult and must be undertaken on a large scale. Pollution control in the home is more feasible, because the space to be considered is enclosed, air movement is artificially induced, and there are efficient air cleaners available which effectively remove most pollutants from the air. This booklet, "Air Cleaning Facts," is designed to acquaint you with in-the-home air pollution control systems.

Send: a postcard
Ask for: "Air Cleaning Facts"
Write to: Research Products Corp.
Madison, Wisc. 53701

energy-saving winter is what this little book is all about.

Send: a postcard
Ask for: "Winter Survival" (DOE/OPA-0019R-2-79)
Write to: DOE Technical Information Center
P.O. Box 62
Oak Ridge, Tenn. 37830

Electrical Current

A handy little 8-page brochure, "Ground Fault Circuit Interrupter," attempts to reduce the number of deaths and injuries every year due to electrical shock from appliances and power tools. The hidden hazard is called "ground fault"—a small amount of current "leaking" to the exposed metal parts of an appliance or a tool. This booklet describes the ground fault circuit interrupter, a device which constantly monitors the electrical current to stop accidents and protect your life.

Ask for: "Ground Fault Circuit Interrupter"
For further information, write to:
National Emergencies Safety Council
444 N. Michigan Ave.
Chicago, Ill. 60611

Home Heating Emergencies

Don't get left out in the cold this winter when some disaster strikes your heating system. "Home Heating in an Emergency" tells you how to plan secondary heating systems, emergency heating areas for your family, and evacuation procedures. Included are explanations of related problems that can occur when your heat goes off and what to about them.
Send: 75¢
Ask for: "Home Heating in an Emergency" (NRAES-9)
Write to: Distribution Center, Dept. FHO
7 Research Park
Cornell University
Ithaca, N.Y. 14850

Child Safety

A booklet devoted to protecting your child in the home is "Your Child and Household Safety" by M. Arena, M.D. Twenty pages discuss those hazards which affect particular periods of childhood, as well as principles of first aid. Remember: accidents kill more children than the five leading fatal diseases combined.
Send: 50¢
Ask for: "Your Child and Household Safety"
Write to: Chemical Specialties Manufacturers Association, Inc.
Suite 1120
1001 Connecticut Ave., N.W.
Washington , D.C. 20036

Your child and household safety

Mothers have never deliberately gone shopping for poisons, but the fact is that they buy several every time they go to the grocery store or market. They use them whenever they clean house, polish the furniture, wash the dishes, paint the kitchen, or clean a spot off their husband's tie.

Healthy Houses

Improve the life expectancy of your house: use preventive medicine! "Finding and Keeping a Healthy Home" tells in 21 pages not only how to select a house that's in tip-top shape, but how to keep it in robust condition. A health checklist aids in detecting first signs of house-sickness.
Send: $1.25
Ask for: "Finding and Keeping a Healthy Home," (#1284)
Write to: U.S. Government Printing Office
Washington, D.C. 20402

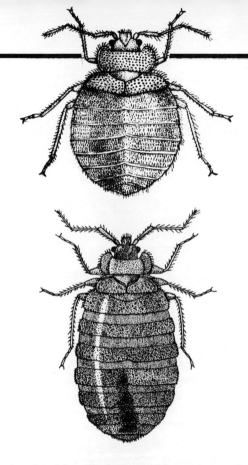

Finding and keeping a healthy home

No buyer is looking for a house that is infested with termites or weakened by rot, but many a buyer gets just that . . . In a poorly constructed house, damage may not be visible. The buyer, therefore, should give careful attention to design features as well as signs of insects or decay.

Fleas

Shoo flea—don't bother me, or my dog, or my cat. A 6-page leaflet, "Controlling Fleas," tells you how to control fleas on your pets, and in your home. Included is a guide for mixing sprays.

Send: 60¢
Ask for: "Controlling Fleas" (121)
Write to: Superintendent of Documents
U.S. Printing Office
Washington, D.C. 20402

Controlling fleas

Don't be alarmed if your dog or cat shows discomfort for a few minutes after the application (of insecticides). Insecticides often cause increased activity by the fleas in their last moments of life. If the animal has free run, treatments may have to be repeated to keep fleas under control . . . If the animal is confined to an area free of fleas, one treatment usually is enough.

Bedbugs

Everyone should have the right to choose their own bed-partners. Unfortunately, bedbugs never take "no" for an answer. Put your foot down with "How to Control Bedbugs." This 8-page booklet teaches you first to recognize evidence of late-night visits and then how to keep those unwelcome intruders away forever.

Send: 70¢
Ask for: "How to Control Bedbugs"
Write to: Superintendent of Documents
Government Printing Office
Washington, D.C. 20402

How to control bed bugs

Bed bugs feed mostly at night by biting people who are asleep. But if they are very hungry and if the light is dim, bed bugs will feed during the day. When bed bugs bite, they inject a fluid into the skin that assists them in obtaining blood. Often the fluid causes the skin to become irritated and inflamed; welts develop and there is much itching.

Cockroaches

Some household animals are pets, others are pests. "Cockroaches—How to Control Them" is a 10-page booklet dealing with the latter.

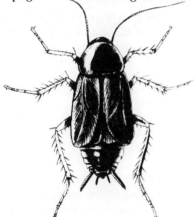

The seven most common roaches and their habitat (yours) are described—but most important, this booklet tells you how to rid your house of these pests.
Send: $1.00
Ask for: "Cockroaches—How to Control Them" (#430)

Write to: U.S. Department of Agriculture
Science and Ed. Adm.
Hyattsville, Md. 20782

Cockroaches: How to control them

Placing a band of dust on the floor around the edges of a room is not an adequate treatment. Many cockroaches may be able to go from their hiding places to sources of food and water without crossing the band of dust.

Termites

Roaches may eat your food, but termites devour your house! In 1970 alone, termites destroyed $500 million worth of property across the country. If these pests are eating you out of house and home, send for the 30-page "Subterranean Termites—Their Prevention and Control in Buildings."
Send: $1.30
Ask for: "Subterranean Termites—Their Prevention and Control in Buildings"
Write to: Superintendent of Documents
U.S. Government Printing Office
Washington, D.C. 20402

You can protect your home from termites

Don't panic! Thankfully, termites are slow eaters. Even a mature, well-established colony of 60,000 workers eats only a fifth of an ounce of wood a day. So take your time. Evaluate your situation. And remember, research by the U.S. Forest Service has made it possible to control termites.

Finances and Family Records

Household Records

When was the last time you couldn't find a passport or birth certificate you knew you had put away carefully someplace? Have you ever wondered how others would go about finding important papers after you die? A government fold-out, "Keeping Family/Household Records," helps you devise and organize a system for storing important records and papers. Includes a checklist chart on what to keep, what to discard.

Send: a postcard
Ask for: "Keeping Family/Household Records" (623H)
Write to: Consumer Information Center
Department Z
Pueblo, Colo. 81009

Keeping family/household records

How long should you keep tax records? The Internal Revenue Service has 3 years in which to audit Federal income tax returns. However, this limit does not apply in unusual cases. If you failed to report more than 25 percent of your gross income, the Government has 6 years to collect the tax or to start legal proceedings. Also, there are no time limitations if you filed a fraudulent return or if you failed to file a return.

Household Inventory

How much do you have to lose? Could you recall all your belongings and determine their worth if fire or burglars struck? If not, send for an Inventory Record from Allstate.

Send: a postcard
Ask for: "Your Household Inventory Record"
Write to: Allstate Insurance
Northbrook, Ill. 60062

Financial Records

Many people think of their financial worth in terms of salary. Few realize the many variables that contribute to the overall financial picture. "Net Worth Statement" explains how to calculate and analyze your net worth and how to use this information. Six pages include an asset worksheet and a liability worksheet.

Send: 25¢
Ask for: "Net Worth Statement" (CEH-6)

Write to: Distribution Center, Dept. FHO
7 Research Park
Cornell University
Ithaca, N.Y. 14850

Family Budget

Many families know they should keep a budget, yet they don't know how to do it successfully. A 14-page booklet, "A Guide to Budgeting for the Family," puts a family in control of the household money flow. Learn to keep charts on family spending, and educate the family on wise spending, buying, and credit practices.

Keeping Records

Send: 35¢
Ask for: "A Guide to Budgeting for the Family" (#108)
Write to: Superintendent of Documents
U.S. Government Printing Office
Washington, D.C. 20402

A guide for budgeting for the family

To use consumer credit wisely, make certain that: You know how much the use of credit costs. You have shopped around and chosen the best available terms. You need the item urgently enough to justify the credit cost.

Valuable Papers

Everyone has important papers he seldom thinks about. Personal health records, financial and insurance papers, deeds, and other property records all play a part in our lives. If any of these papers were needed for an emergency, could you find them quickly? "Do You Know Your Valuable Papers?" helps you locate, inventory, and index your papers. Eight pages are filled with inventories and lists that help evaluate all necessary information.

Send: 25¢
Ask for: "Do You Know Your Valuable Papers?" (E-963)
Write to: Distribution Center, Dept. FHO
7 Research Park
Cornell University
Ithaca, N.Y. 14850

Electric Bills

If you feel helpless about your growing elec-

tric bill, put yourself back in charge with "111 Ways to Control Your Electric Bill." This booklet points out those hidden leaks where you may be losing expensive electricity through faulty appliances, poorly installed windows and doors, and careless energy habits. For instance: do you turn out extra lights, but neglect dripping hot-water faucets? Even cooking is affected: one-dish meals are cheaper than multi-course dinners; the shape of pans, and even checking your roast too often, all total up to a higher electric bill.

Send: a postcard
Ask for: "111 Ways to Control Your Electric Bill"
Write to: your local utility company

Electric Bills

To most homeowners, the electric company is just an invisible entity demanding monthly payments for a service we tend to take for granted. To better understand what really goes on at the electric company, especially in relation to your utility bills, send for "You and Your Electric Company," 36 pages with charts and diagrams.

Send: a postcard
Ask for: "You and Your Electric Company"
Write to: Edison Electric Institute
1140 Connecticut Ave., N.W.
Washington, D.C. 20036

111 ways to control your electric bill
Direct sunlight falling on a window air-conditioning unit

increases its work load. When a choice is possible, locate such units on the north or shady side of the house.

Mortgages

When you can't make your mortgage payments, who can help? "Having Problems Paying Your Mortgage?" will point out important facts to consider, what to avoid, recommend private and public agencies to assist you and even define the legal terms used in discussing your situation.

Send: a postcard
Ask for: "Having Problems Paying Your Mortgage?"
Write to: Consumer Information Center
Department Z
Pueblo, Colo. 81009

Frauds

An alarming number of individuals and companies in the home improvement field rip off millions of dollars each year from unsuspecting homeowners. Don't be a victim! Decide in advance just what it is that you want done and how much you can afford to spend; check all references, and get all promises in writing! These, and many more, words to the wise are

included in "Home Improvement Frauds," a fold-out from the U.S. Department of Justice.

Send: a postcard
Ask for: "Home Improvement Frauds"
Write to: National District Attorney's Association
666 N. Lake Shore Dr. Suite 1432
Chicago, Ill. 60611

Home improvement frauds

How to be "Ripped Off" for Sure:

1. Hire a high-pressure door-to-door salesperson.
2. Insist on a verbal contract. Read nothing. Sign every form he gives you.
3. Pay cash in advance.
4. Go on vacation while job is in progress. Give the contractor a key.
5. Ignore lien statements that are received.
6. Be too embarrassed to complain to your local district attorney.

Credit Shopping

The Annual Percentage Rate is the rate you pay per dollar per year for credit you use. The Finance Charge is the total dollar amount you are charged for that credit. To compute what your loan or mortgage is costing you, check the "Credit Shopping Guide."

Send: $1.00
Ask for: "Credit Shopping Guide" (M-01-1)
Write to: Superintendent of Documents
U.S. Government Printing Office
Washington, D.C. 20402

Inflation

With everyone feeling the inflationary pinch these days, many consumers wonder about the origins of inflation and what can be done to curb its growth. "Your Inflation Guide: Dollars and Sense" gives a concise, readable definition of inflation and explores some of the causes. Eleven pages offer explanations of causes and effects, a summary of how government can restrain growth, and advice on how you, the consumer, can help in the fight against inflation.

Send: a postcard
Ask for: "Your Inflation Guide: Dollars and Sense"
Write to: Dollars and Sense
Pueblo, Colo. 81009

Crafts and Hobbies

Wood Crafts

For a wealth of woodworking materials, send for "Constantine's 1981 Woodworker's Catalog." Here you'll find all sorts of woods, tools, refinishing materials, mouldings, carvings, furniture patterns, veneer inlays, etc. For those interested in refinishing furniture there are clamps, brass hinges, antique pulls, ceramic knobs, box locks, and more.

Send: $1.00
Ask for: "Constantine's 1981 Woodworker's Catalog"
Write to: Constantine
2050 Eastchester Road
Bronx, N.Y. 10761

Wood Finishing

Beauty, ease of maintenance, and lasting protection have made natural wood finishing one of the most popular decorating trends in today's homes. A 24-page booklet, "A Short Course in Natural Wood Finishing," gives you the basic principles of natural wood finishing. Produce the warm and mellow look you love without professional assistance. Wood and finish selection, surface preparation informa-tion, and staining procedures are all included.

Send: 75¢
Ask for: "A Short Course in Natural Wood Finishing"
Write to: Pierce and Stevens Chemical Corp.
P.O. Box 1092
Buffalo, N.Y. 14240

Refinishing

Whatever it is you want to refinish—walls, doors, floors, pianos, beds or boats—"Latest and Best Methods in Refinishing" will show how to do it. Removing varnish, paint, wallpaper, preparing surfaces, applying the new finish, even how to care for and clean brushes —all these procedures are made easy in this complete guide.

Send: 50¢
Ask for: "Latest and Best Methods in Refinishing"
Write to: Wilson-Imperial Co.
115 Chestnut St.
Newark, N.J. 07105

Picture Frames

How better to enhance a favorite picture or painting than to build your own frame? A booklet called "Fun-to-Make Picture Frames" shows you how to measure, cut, and assemble your own frame, and offers 39 molding patterns to choose from. You'll also learn glazing, metal leafing, matting, lining, mounting, backing, hanging, grouping, finishing, and how to build a lattice frame.

Send: 60¢
Ask for: "Fun-to-Make Picture Frames"
Write to: Western Wood Moulding and
Millwork Producers
P.O. Box 25278
Portland, Ore. 97225

Fun to make picture frames

The final step in the frame making is the hanging of the picture. Screw eyes are the most common fastener used for hanging pictures. The screw eyes should be a length that is about ¾ as thick as the frame. It is a good idea to use a small pilot hole to prevent splitting the frame. Fasten the screw eyes on the strongest part of the frame. Measure ⅓ of the distance down from the top and place the screw eyes.

night and spin hardly-noticeable webs. Leaves of the plant will turn dull green or gray and foliage surfaces are stippled.

Houseplants

"How often should I water my plants?" "Why are my leaves turning yellow?" These are some of the many questions asked by aspiring indoor gardeners. "Houseplants," a 52-page booklet from *Better Homes and Gardens*, solves common plant problems and offers ideas for growing succulents, ferns, flowering favorites, forced bulbs, and even terrariums.

Send: $1.25
Ask for: "Houseplants"
Write to: National Plan Service
435 W. Fullerton Ave.
Elmhurst, Ill. 60126

Houseplants

Spider mites descend on houseplants like thieves in the

Pet Care

All the facts you need to know for selecting, training and living with a cat or dog are in these two little books from Ralston Purina. Histories of the animals, housebreaking techniques, health care requirements, teaching tricks, acquiring a second or third pet, plus answers to many common questions asked by pet owners are explained with charts and illustrations.

Send: 25¢ each
Ask for: "Handbook of Cat Care"
  "Handbook of Dog Care"
Write to: Ralston Purina Cat &
  Dog Care Center
  Checkerboard Square
  St. Louis, Mo. 63188

Handbook of dog care (cat care)

Worms are internal parasites. External parasites are fleas, lice, ticks, and mites . . . Fleas not only make your dog's life miserable, but act to bring on more formidable problems such as tapeworms or lead to allergies.

Cooking Tips

"Cooking Cleverly" is a cookbook with an ingenious plan for gas range users: save energy by cooking entire meals in one place! This may mean "tuna and macaroni casserole siciliana" on the top burners, "chicken breasts" in the oven, or "barbecued beef steaks" in the broiler. Be smart, save money, but eat well!

Send: 65¢
Ask for: "Cooking Cleverly"
Write to: American Gas Association
  1515 Wilson Blvd.
  Arlington, Va. 22209

Cooking cleverly

One-place cooking might have been invented for the oven. The oven is so versatile and often so roomy, that it should just naturally encourage you to plan whole meals around its use.

Quilts and Needles

The exquisite "Stearns and Foster Catalog of

Quilt Pattern Designs and Needle Craft Supplies" boasts 129 beautiful line drawings of quilt patterns. Even if you don't use the basic instructions to make a quilt or comforter, you'll enjoy learning to identify traditional and modern quilt designs and patterns.

Send: $1.50
Ask for: "Stearns and Foster Catalog of Quilt Pattern Designs and Needle Craft Supplies"
Write to: Stearns and Foster Co.
Wyoming and Williams St.
Cincinnati, Ohio 45215

Velcro

A material using the same sticking qualities as the natural burr is the subject of "The Velcro Revolution Starts Here." This 7-page pamphlet will give you decorating ideas for fashion, home, car, and even dog. A cute extra is a sew-it-yourself pattern for a change purse.
Send: a postcard

Ask for: "The Velcro Revolution Starts Here"
Write to: Velcro U.S.A. Inc.
521 Fifth Ave.
New York, N.Y. 10175

Wool

If we only treated it right, wool could go on forever. It's certainly worth it: wool is durable, absorbent, flame-resistant, wrinkle-resistant, color-fast, resilient and beautiful! And unlike manmade fibers, wool breathes with our bodies. "Tender Loving Care for Wool," a fold-out from the American Wool Council, tells you how to give wool the attention it deserves to keep it looking its best.
Send: 15¢
Ask for: "Tender Loving Care for Wool"
Write to: Wool Education Center
200 Clayton St.
Denver, Colo. 80206

A Special Bonus Offer

Do It Yourself

Why fret a day or longer for a repairman and then pay outrageous wages? You can save time and money today by doing your own minor household repairs or auto tuneups...and have fun at the same time! Even "lazy" homeowners can learn to do tasks they've never tackled before with these fully illustrated, step-by-step handbooks for a variety of simple home maintenance and auto care jobs. Each book, written by an expert in the field in language the average homeowner can understand, includes a shopping list for all the necessary tools and equipment.

Send: 50¢ each*

Ask for: "How to Fix a Leak and Other Household Plumbing Projects"

"How to Redo Your Kitchen Cabinets and Counter Tops"

"How to Wire Electrical Outlets, Switches and Lights"

"How to Wallpaper"

"How to Build a Deck"

"How to Paint Interiors"

"How to Tune Your Toyota Corolla"

"How to Tune Your Chevy Chevette"

Write to: C.C. Mayer
Cornerstone Library
Simon & Schuster
1230 Avenue of the Americas
New York, N.Y. 10020

*One per household.